THE EVERETT STERN STORY

DARK MONEY AND PRIVATE SPIES

EVERETT STERN

Design and distribution by Bublish, Inc.
Published by Everett Stern

ISBN: 978-1-64704-579-1 (eBook)
ISBN: 978-1-64704-578-4 (paperback)

DEDICATION

This book is dedicated to every friend that has supported me through good times and bad. Without every hardship, challenge, success and accomplishment this book would not have been possible. A special thanks to my Angels Janet and Valerie.

FOREWORD

I am honored to write the foreword for this book about my friend and colleague, Everett Stern. At its core, this is a true-life story about how one man challenged an international corporate banking giant that was facilitating the movement of terrorist money around the globe. Everett paid a steep price in his personal and professional life. He then picked up the pieces of his life, worked hard, and formed and successfully developed a private security and intelligence company—one that he currently runs today.

On one level, this is the ultimate American success story—a man who builds up his life, takes a principled stand on an important issue, gets knocked down, and then gets back up again and rebuilds his life to even greater levels of success. On a separate level, this is a story of how one person can make a significant difference on an important issue that is facing our country. We have a saying in our line of work: "Many are called, few are chosen." Everett heard the call and not only answered it but did so in a singular and impressive fashion. While the US intelligence community was focused on the issue of how international and domestic terrorist groups were moving their money around to fund their terrorist operations after 9/11, we did not fully comprehend the level of complicity that many US and international banks and some of their selected officials had in terrorist money laundering effort. Everett was one of a rare handful of individuals who not only noticed that some of these big banks were wittingly moving funds from designated terrorist individuals and groups but took forceful and aggressive action to stop this illicit behavior, with the ultimate objective of trying to save innocent lives and make our country a safer place. When HSBC refused to change its practices despite Everett's discovery of illegal activity, he made the conscious decision to discreetly provide this information to the pertinent US authorities. In the end, HSBC was fined a record $1.92 billion. However, no officials were held accountable—another intriguing aspect of this story—demonstrating the apparent "coziness" between elements of the United States government and major banking and financial institutions.

I have a deep admiration and respect for Everett and the critical role he played in helping illuminate terrorist money laundering at a major international bank. Not many people on this planet would have the courage, fortitude, intelligence, and strong sense of morals and ethics to do what he did. He has remained true to his core beliefs and sense of justice, integrity, and doing what is right at his position as founder and CEO of his private security and intelligence company, Tactical Rabbit. Everett and Tactical Rabbit take on clients who have been wronged in some way and who need the capabilities and advocacy of his company to right an injustice.

I only wish that this country had more men like Everett who were willing to use their unique skill set to right what is wrong and to take principled, moral, and just stands on the myriad of threats and issues that face us here in the Homeland. I am humbled to call Everett both a personal friend and a professional colleague in this ongoing struggle against all forms of injustice and extremism. Please enjoy this true-life story of an unsung American hero.

Bob Dougherty CIA (Retired)

CONTENTS

INTRODUCTION

Modern-day mathematics and physics are defined by the concept of infinity. Even something that is defined by "absolute" boundaries is infinite. For example, calculus is based on the notion that an object can be divided up an infinite number of times, because you can always divide something in half no matter how small it is. I started thinking about the concept of infinity in relation to the disillusionment that American society faces. I have come to the conclusion that freedom and justice are defined by the facts, not absolutes. Not everyone is free. Justice does not always prevail—a fact that has become my greatest motivation.

I'll be the first to admit that I thought HSBC Bank being brought to justice was an absolute. Unfortunately, we all know the reality of what happened in that money laundering scandal: the bad guys got away. There was no justice. No dove flew across the courtroom. This result begs the question: If the essence of America, in the form of freedom and justice, are not absolutes, then why should we believe in them?

Our founding fathers created the essence of American freedom and justice because they believed they were worth fighting for. No matter how many HSBC terrorist-financing bankers get away, no matter how many times our freedom is infringed upon or the justice system fails us, we must continue fighting for the "American absolutes" that will, by their very nature, never be absolute. It is the caring, the struggle, and the fight that make us American. I'm proud to say that I cared, I struggled, and I fought for justice. Every victory brought an overwhelming sense of humility. Every loss prepared me for the next battle.

THE BEST JOB OF MY LIFE

I started at HSBC on October 10, 2010. I was a man on a self-directed mission to bring about justice. There was one problem, though: I had no idea how to do my job as an Anti-Money Laundering Compliance Officer. But that wasn't going to stop me. All I needed to do was learn everything about how to uncover and track the money flows of terrorists and drug cartels—and my dad had ingrained in me from birth that I could teach myself anything with books. In preparation for my new job at HSBC, and throughout my tenure, I read. I read every morning before walking into work. And, at home, I sat at my little desk in my Delaware apartment and read. Once a day, I would even show my higher-ups the books so they would see how much I was learning. But their response was less than positive.

"Just focus on your job. Close more alerts," they would say, consistently blowing me off. It only made me try harder.

I went into this job with purpose and meaning, excited to make a difference. I had the responsibility to ensure terrorists did not launder money through the bank. But my exuberance was met with harsh resistance.

From day one, my direct supervisor hated me. There was zero training, so I chalked it up to her being annoyed with mistakes made by "the new guy." I always asked her questions, raised numerous concerns, and wanted to escalate my alerts to Suspicious Activity Reports (SARs). But she consistently blew me off and often boasted about how much experience she had as a debt collector— the person who calls you to collect a debt when you default on your HSBC credit card. HSBC determined that she was the perfect fit to head the financial intelligence unit at the bank. I guess having twenty-five years of experience as a debt collector was just what HSBC wanted—someone whose only real understanding of compliance was getting people to cough up a couple hundred bucks to pay off their couch. I can't fault her for taking the job as the Head of Financial Intelligence for the Correspondent Banking Division for International HSBC Wires; HSBC hired her for the same reason the executives I nicknamed "Traitor" and "Burns" hired me—neither one of us knew what we were doing.

> **SAR**
> Suspicious Activity Report is a financial intelligence transaction that is halted. A list is made of the originator and the beneficiary with their risk rating. The SAR is sent to the Treasury Department and other government agencies.
> HSBC lowered the risk ratings to allow illegal transactions to go through and accrue financial benefits.

They thought I was some schmuck who was going to sit in my cubicle, marinating in a $54,900 salary. It became very apparent to me on day one that I was not hired to make a difference. I was hired to click my mouse and close alerts, which in turn allowed terrorists and drug cartel money to kill people. Dramatic? Overstatement? Absolutely not. HSBC designed a compliance system full of unqualified people who had no idea what they were doing to defraud the United States government and its people. I was outraged. Ultimately, they were killing people.

You may ask, "How can a bank kill people?" Wars cost money. Bullets cost money. Bombs cost money. Wars are fought and won with the almighty dollar. Did you know HSBC Bank was involved in financing 9/11? I am not going to recite a history lesson on HSBC, but do your homework and you will see HSBC has financed our enemies and is responsible for American deaths. Think I'm joking? Once I blew the whistle on HSBC, the bank actually admitted guilt in federal documents and plead guilty to "financing the enemy."

Was I qualified to be an Anti-Money Laundering Compliance Officer? No, I was far from qualified. Everyone there was unqualified. That is the point. Many of the same people with whom I worked are still working there now, approving transactions—hence, money going to terrorists and drug cartels. My job at HSBC was to close alerts. This is how it worked.

My department handled all of the international wires for HSBC. This did not occur in HSBC North America HQ, but in New Castle, Delaware. As an example, say you bank with J.P. Morgan and want to send $10,000 to your cousin in Gambia, Africa, who banks with Standard Chartered. How do you get it there? There are no J.P. Morgan banks in Gambia, and let's say J.P. Morgan has no relationship with Standard Chartered.

This is where correspondent banking comes in. HSBC has a massive international presence. HSBC is all over the world, including countries that are enemies of the United States, like Iran. But in the Gambia case, HSBC has a correspondent relationship with Standard Chartered, which is in Gambia. So, you initiate the wire with J.P. Morgan, and J.P. Morgan sends it to HSBC, which then sends it to Standard Chartered in Gambia.

HSBC is the world's conduit for other banks. And HSBC's correspondent banking also works the other way around. Overseas HSBC account holders were sending money from one HSBC account to another in a different country. Basically, my department handled a large percentage of the world's wire transfers. Many of the terrorist-related wires I saw also involved other banks, with HSBC orchestrating them all.

HSBC makes a fortune from acting as the world's wire broker. It's not in HSBC's interest to stop these wires. People don't realize that the fine of $1.92 billion related to my evidence was just a cost of doing business. The fine amounted to only five weeks of profit. The banks are happy to pay these fines because, in the end, they are still very profitable.

Norkom
A financial compliance alert monitoring system, that allows for mass clearance of alerts.
Used by HSBC to circumvent US sanctions on terrorists and drug dealers.

Now, say you're a terrorist and you need to get money to multiple cells across the world or in various cities in a particular country, for bomb-making materials and weapons. You initiate twelve wires, each at $9,999, to every person, through either HSBC or a correspondent bank that HSBC is controlling. An alert will be generated in the HSBC Alert Monitoring System (before a new software came out called Norkom). On my computer screen in my little cubicle, I will see an alert, which is just a numbered code (for example, #1234), which is assigned to me. So, I have the Alert Monitoring System software program open on my HSBC computer, and in the "Everett Stern" file, a little folder pops up with my number. I open the file, and the details of the alert are there. I see who sent the wire (called the *originator*), then who received the wire (known as *beneficiaries*), and the respective dollar amount sent to each person from the originator.

In this case, it's all the same amount of $9,999. Now, this number is significant because it is what's called "under the trigger." Any time you wire the rounded number of $10,000, it has to be reported to the Treasury. Bad guys do not want to be reported, so they will wire under $10,000. If the originator is sending multiple wires at around the same amount to multiple beneficiaries, it is considered a red flag. Another key element I would see in the alert—besides the originator, beneficiaries, dollar amounts, and the banks involved—is the country. This is where things get interesting and the laws of compliance physics began to bend.

HSBC has its own country ratings. Where they got these ratings, I have no idea, but certain countries (like Mexico) are considered low risk. The way it works, for example, is like this: An HSBC customer in Saudi Arabia (regarded as high-risk country), wires money to another HSBC customer in Lebanon (another high-risk country). If an alert is generated, we are told it is to be immediately closed and to allow the transaction through. The reason being the transaction is going from one HSBC account to other HSBC accounts and the HSBC reps and bankers have already vetted the originator and beneficiaries.

Really let that sink in. Our supervisor created all kinds of rules regarding alerts, which came directly from the HSBC North America CEO in New York. Fixing the game to defraud the United States was a "from the top down" approach.

Looking back at my computer screen, I would have to be sure there was enough to escalate the case. Every time I moved forward, my bosses would bust my balls

> **OFAC**
> The Office of Foreign Assets Control is a financial intelligence and enforcement agency of the U.S. Treasury Department.
> It administers and enforces economic and trade sanctions against individuals and entities that are threats to U.S. national security and foreign policy objectives.
> US companies are banned from doing business with them.

and give me a hard time, so I'd try to make my case even more solid by researching the beneficiaries who received the moneys. We had tools like World-Check and LexisNexis, but we were never trained on LexisNexis, so nobody used it. World-Check was an internet-based site. We inputted a name, and the software tried to match the name with known criminals and terrorists—specifically, people on the Office of Foreign Assets Controls (OFAC) sanctions list.

If I typed in the name Osama bin Laden, a million matches would come up. This was the problem with World-Check. Common names, especially Arabic names, could not be identified as the person in the wire because there were too many matches. This meant I was stymied from taking any action with almost every alert. HSBC didn't use World-Check to help determine if someone was a terrorist. They just wanted us to run the name, take a PDF of whatever matched the result, and then attach it to the alert. They wanted to show the government regulators—whom I never saw the entire time I worked there—that an effort was made. The same thing applied to LexisNexis. Names were run, and we always got the same screen with a list of names that we could do nothing with.

In one specific alert case, I ran World-Check and LexisNexis hoping to nail something because I knew the wires contained in the alert were questionable.

I ran to my supervisor. "I have a ton of World-Check and LexisNexis names. How do I identify the person in my wire?"

"Everett, just PDF it and attach it. Close the damn alert and move on. You have another twenty-five to do today."

She was right. I had twenty-five more to do. All compliance officers had to keep track of the time spent on each alert. Why? Because the alerts kept coming. There was so much criminal and terrorist activity running through the bank that the bank could not keep up. The quota of alerts changed month by month, but at one point, there were one hundred fifty thousand alerts back-logged. We had to complete over one hundred a week.

I stapled the bullshit PDF to the alert, but I decided to make one last-ditch effort. *Google.* This was the ultimate resource. The key for me was to try to find a connection from the people named in the wires to the companies. Once I found the link to a company, I could search the news and try to find some terrorist or drug cartel link. When I did find a link—say in Lebanon—in all of my youthful, twenty-five-year-old excitement, I dashed over to a cubicle a few rows ahead, where I found my supervisor chatting with an underqualified employee, blowing bubbles with her gum, as she nodded in agreement to something she probably didn't understand. "Ma'am, I found a link to a company in Lebanon. I need more time on this alert."

"Everett, how many alerts have you closed today?"

"Five."

"You don't have time to write a SAR. Close it and catch up."

A SAR is the ultimate intelligence weapon for the Treasury department. If a compliance officer working for a United States bank sees something that is suspicious, the law requires that it be reported to the Treasury in a SAR. A SAR is an electronic PDF that is filled out in a very similar fashion to a police report. The compliance officer is notifying the Treasury of all of the facts found in the case so the US government can take action. What action? If my alert with the beneficiaries linked to a company in Lebanon turns out to be a terrorist cell about to hijack a plane, the information I wrote in the SAR that went to a Treasury official is then sent to the FBI and CIA to take action. Banking Suspicious Activity Reports are critical to providing the FBI and CIA the intelligence needed to protect the United States.

I went back to my cubical, defeated, and stared at the alert, which I was going to be forced to close. Then I stared at the framed poem my dad had given me to hang in my cubicle:

> What is success? To laugh often and much; To win the respect of intelligent people and the affection of children; To earn the appreciation of honest critics and endure the betrayal of false friends; To appreciate the beauty; To find the best in others; To leave the world a bit better, whether by a healthy child, a garden patch or a redeemed social condition; To know even one life has breathed easier because you have lived; This is to have succeeded. — Ralph Waldo Emerson

I shook my head and closed the alert. I began the excruciating cycle of going to management only to be told forget it and move on. At twenty-five years old, I was a kid—a very scared kid—and I didn't know if what I was seeing was real. I closed alerts multiple times a day for almost a month. I knew the process was harmful to the United States and I was potentially helping terrorists with every alert I was forced to close. It felt like pointing a gun at an American soldier's head and pulling the trigger; with every alert I closed, I imagined the coffin of a fallen American soldier.

I should have gotten out of my cubicle and left immediately. But, again, I was twenty-five, second-guessing myself, and feeling powerless. Plus, my parents were finally proud of me. I was making $55K a year. I had an apartment and a car. I was stable. For once, I thought, maybe I needed to keep my mouth shut. My hesitation is something I will regret until my last day on this earth. Finally, I couldn't take it anymore. I knew what I had to do, but I also knew it would mean that my life would never be the same.

After work, I sped home to my apartment. I called my mom and dad and told them what was going on. My parents, out of complete worry for their child, advised me to keep my mouth shut. They were seriously concerned for my safety, and they didn't want to see me on the streets without a job. But I knew if my dad had seen what I had, he would do something. His advice was given out of fear. Any parent would be very concerned in a situation like this. I hung up the phone with them and paced around my apartment. If I kept digging, it was possible I would lose my job— or worse, get killed.

Nighttime fell upon me as I was still thinking about my course of action. I had to be at work at 9:00 the next morning. There was no dinner, just bed. I felt sick to my stomach. I lay in the darkness with my eyes closed, imagining myself about to jump off a cliff. As I plummeted to the sharp rocks below, with the aggressive waves crashing over them, I opened my eyes and knew the course of action. I got out of bed at about 1:00 a.m. and went to my computer.

On November 7, 2010, at 2:01:10 a.m. EST, I emailed a CIA recruiter, I had interviewed with years earlier. *I have intelligence to provide to the CIA regarding money laundering. I am currently working as an anti-money laundering officer for a foreign bank.*

THE MAD TEA PARTY:
INMATES RUNNING THE ASYLUM

HSBC became my own personal war—which continues to this day and will continue for the rest of my life. I didn't "blow the whistle" and walk away from the situation. I initially fought to be the best the employee I could be. Then, after realizing that HSBC management wanted me to be the worst Anti-Money Laundering Officer known to man, I set my sights on a higher purpose.

I sat in my little cubicle, checking my email. The Treasury department sent out emails to the compliance officers of the updated OFAC sanctions list (i.e., a list of people and companies banned from doing business by the United States Government).

Even though HSBC is a foreign bank, they still have a major subsidiary— HSBC North America—headquartered in New York. This meant that any transaction going through New Castle, Delaware, to my department, had to comply with the OFAC sanctions list. The OFAC sanctions list was made up of the worst terrorists and their affiliated companies, Russian mobsters, and cartel members. The list was always being updated because some new company was linked to helping or financing terrorism. Being on the OFAC sanctions list was a financial death sentence because that meant no money could be moved. But the terrorists and drug cartels found a loophole—HSBC Bank.

For months, I repeatedly went to management, ringing the alarm bells when I saw a banking transaction that related to "Foreign Terrorist Organizations." My calls for help were ignored, and, eventually, HSBC management tried to silence me with a possible HR issue. The senior manager actually said to me, "Hamas is not a terrorist organization," and went on to say, "Well, Stern, it looks like you have a problem with Muslims." I knew what he was doing; he was suggesting that I was racist and trying to covertly threaten me with the sort of HR disciplinary action that could render me jobless. What he failed to understand was that I knew there was a difference between Muslims and terrorists. Most religious people are peaceful and simply want to make the world a better place by connecting to a higher power. There are, however, slivers and factions that hijack religion and use the ideology for war. Throughout history, there have been terrorist groups, domestic and foreign, from all religions. I knew the office politics management was trying to play. I was a chess player, and I saw on the board how they were going to try to call checkmate. Unfortunately for management, their plan to paint me as a Muslim-hating banking officer hit a snag when another manager made a questionable move. During a heated conversation with me, she blurted out, "Everett, you should wear a yellow star around the office."

Yes. I am serious. Word for word.

The comment was made, and other people heard it. I launched an HR complaint, and the manager admitted to the comment. A manager told a Jewish employee to wear the star that his ancestors were forced to wear by the Nazis in Germany. What was the HSBC corporate action? An apology. No firing. Nothing. I didn't care. I knew the types I was dealing with. I had to stay focused. My mission was to stop terrorist financing on American soil. About midway through my tenure at HSBC, I discovered that I was not alone on the journey.

"Nobody talks to the press!" The words echoed through the office and sent a chill up my spine. The feeling of panic was palpable. My supervisor stumbled, half running into the boss's "office," which was basically just a cubicle larger than the rest of ours. I immediately left my desk and went to the front entrance of the building, hoping to see tons of TV cameras and reporters. I wanted so badly for HSBC to be exposed for the crimes it was committing. But I knew I couldn't talk to the press, not yet, because it would interfere with my primary objective, which was to ascertain as much incriminating information as possible.

I saw that the obese security guard was actually up on his feet, huffing and puffing for oxygen like he had done a lap around a shopping mall.

I asked, "Where are the reporters? The parking lot is empty."

"That idiot was out back in the dumpster."

"In the dumpster?"

"Yeah, trying to get documents."

Nobody knew his name or what news agency he was from. It was not until I left HSBC and after I went to the FBI that I actually met the dumpster diver, but his nickname among reporters was "Cougar."

I spent the next few months gathering more evidence that I secretly hoped would take them down. During that time, I questioned every choice I made. In my gut, I thought I was doing the right thing, but I also wondered if it would make any difference at all. But every time I was about to lose my sense of purpose, another piece of the puzzle fell into place.

A good example of that is the day I found evidence of blatant manipulation of the system. I remember looking at the OFAC list, scanning it over, when an interesting name caught my eye: Tajco.

After some simple Google searches, I read that Tajco was a company in Lebanon that supposedly did construction but was actually a front for Hezbollah. Tajco Company also owned Kairaba Supermarket, which was a grocery chain throughout Northern and Western Africa. I went back to the OFAC sanctions list and saw Kairaba Supermarket on it.

I was still trying to be the best HSBC employee there ever was, so I opened up a software program on my computer called the

Wire Filter
A customized alert program with every transaction or wire that passes through HSBC.

Wire Filter, which looked like an excel spreadsheet and was very basic due to being managed by unqualified debt collectors. The Wire Filter contained the names on the OFAC sanction list. So, if a wire was sent or received, it would be stopped and forwarded to the HSBC OFAC department, which was a group of brain-dead, comatose patients sitting in their cubicles, doing whatever HSBC told them to do. The key takeaway here is that OFAC-listed names went into the Wire Filter and those wires were never supposed to go through, ever.

I copied Tajco and pasted it into the Customer Account Monitoring Program System (CAMP). I yawned as I waited for the system to process the request, expecting no transactions to appear on my screen. My cursor was still a spinning wheel, indicating that it was processing.

I mumbled, "What the hell is taking so long?"

I was about to restart my computer, thinking the archaic HSBC machine was, yet again, frozen. Then something happened. My screen filled with transactions. I thought there must be something wrong because nothing was supposed to come up. I looked closely at the transactions' originator and beneficiary, and I saw Tajco and Kairaba Supermarket.

"What the hell?" I said quietly to myself, to prevent my drone coworkers from figuring out what I was doing. I even popped my head up out of my cubicle to make sure my bosses were nowhere to be seen. There were hundreds of millions of dollars of Hezbollah funds moving through the bank. It didn't make sense to me. How could Hezbollah wire money through HSBC Bank? I saw the Hezbollah OFAC-sanctioned names in the Wire Filter. I reopened it on my monitor. That's when I saw it. Tajco was spelled Taj.co. It took one dot to beat the system. The Wire Filter only matched exact names. I checked other names in the Wire Filter and they had dashes and periods in them as well. HSBC Bank was manipulating the Wire Filter names, or changing the code, so the name in the wire would not match the Wire Filter. HSBC Bank was criminally and intentionally manipulating the code on the wires so the payments would go through.

OFAC sanctions were ignored at HSBC Bank. This is why, as part of the Deferred Prosecution Agreement where HSBC was fined $1.92 billion, HSBC admitted to the Federal offense of "Financing the Enemy." Luckily for HSBC, they are a major part of our financial system, so they just got fined. If you or I "Financed the Enemy" by giving money to Hezbollah, ISIS, or Hamas, we could be executed. This is one of the many violations I uncovered and submitted to the CIA, and later to the FBI, during my self-directed investigation while working at HSBC.

MONEY LAUNDERING 101

Have you ever played the game Telephone? One person starts a message and whispers it once to the person next to them. That person whispers what they heard to the next person, and so on. After the message is spread all the way around to the last in the group, it often ends up unrecognizable and humorous. Minus the humor, that is the basic premise for money laundering. If you keep moving money from one account to another, from one bank to another, from one currency to another, or from one country to another, its origin is almost impossible to determine.

The dictionary definition of *money laundering* is the process of taking the proceeds of criminal activity and making them appear legal. When the average person thinks of the word laundering, they might envision a white T-shirt on which a splotch of orange spaghetti sauce boldly stands out. It needs to be pretreated, soaked, bleached, cleaned, and perhaps cleaned again. Only after all of this effort would one bother to put the shirt on. Nobody wants to be seen wearing a dirty or stained shirt.

Money obtained illegally is viewed in the same way: It needs to be laundered to remove the proverbial stain, but the downside of dirty money is far greater than being labeled slovenly. The farther the money is moved from its origin, the less recognizable its stain, and the less likely its holder is to be subject to prosecution. Large transactions send up a big red flag, so when one is laundering money, it's essential to break it up into transactions that are smaller than $10,000. According to the Bank Secrecy Act of 1970, the federal government requires banks to report cash transactions of $10,000 or more that are performed in a single day by a single depositor. Another way of avoiding this red flag is to attach the dirty money to a deposit of legitimate funds. For example, a busy auto repair shop, known as *the front*, is making a weekly deposit of $12,000. The owner, who is also making drug money on the side, adds $8,000 from his drug profits to his deposit for a grand total of $20,000. This disguises the drug money and keeps it from appearing dirty.

So where else besides drug sales does dirty money come from? Any illegal money that need to be spent without suspicion constitute dirty money. Arms smugglers, tax evaders, embezzlers, white-collar criminals, and funders of terrorism are just some of the criminals who need their money laundered. Even an ex-spouse might launder some cash to keep it from coming to the attention of his ex-wife. Perhaps a person wants to hide normally taxable income from the IRS to avoid the steep tax payments.

There are generally three steps in laundering large amounts of cash: placement, layering, and integration. Placement is the riskiest step of the laundering process, since large amounts of cash can obviously be conspicuous. The money needs to be deposited into a legitimate bank account without raising suspicion. This often involves large amounts of smaller bills divided in amounts of less than the dreaded $10,000 red flag amount. *Smurfing* is the term used for breaking up funds into less conspicuous amounts. (Yes, it does originate from the small creatures of television fame.) Depending on the amount of cash that needs to be placed, it may take several days, several people, and several different banks to finally "place" the funds. This can be avoided by placing the dirty money in accounts in countries that have fewer and more lenient cash deposit regulations. Some countries have laws that allow anonymous banking. Offshore banks are located outside the depositor's home country and provide low or no-tax advantages. They may not report to other agencies and provide better privacy. This is why they are so frequently associated with organized crime, tax evasion, and money laundering. If you want to hide some cash, check out the banks in the Cayman Islands, Switzerland, the Bahamas, and Luxembourg, to name just a few. It is believed that offshore is where most of the world's drug money is laundered.

The second step of the laundering process is layering. This is the Telephone game, times one hundred. Sometimes dozens of transactions occur to move the money from its original financial institution. It may go from pesos to yen to dollars; from Banco de México to Shoko Chukin Bank to Bank of America. The launderer will do anything possible to make the paper trail impossible to track. Another way of achieving this goal is to use the funds to make purchases. Buying expensive items such as jewelry, cars, and houses changes the form of the money but not the value.

Integration is the final step that brings the money back to usable funds. It may look like income from a cash transfer, investment, or the sale of a high-end product such as diamonds or real estate when it reaches this stage. If the launderer has done his job, he can now use the money without threat of confiscation or prosecution.

So where did the term *money laundering* originate? Some believe that it came from the enormous sums of cash that gangsters were hiding in their fronts: laundromats. The Mafia made much of their fortune from prostitution, gambling, bootlegging liquor, and other such unsavory actions. It is said that Al Capone purchased this high-cash business to help launder his dirty loot. Others believe the term is derived from simply cleaning up dirty money. Al Capone must have been a pro at laundering, since his final conviction in 1931 was simply for tax evasion and not for the crimes that racked up all of his net worth. It is believed that Al Capone laundered $1 billion through a variety of businesses.

Al Capone was not the only famous money launderer of the twentieth century. Bertolt Brecht, the German poet, playwright, and Marxist once said, "If you want to steal, then buy a bank." It seems to be the easiest way of laundering money and making a fortune in the process. The Bank of Credit and Commerce International (BCCI) made the list of the ten most notorious money laundering cases of the twentieth century. BCCI was, at one time, the seventh-largest private bank in the entire world. Among some of its customers were Manuel Noriega, Saddam Hussein, and the Palestinian terrorist Abu Nidal. In the 1980s, the BCCI was investigated and found to be laundering billions of dollars in drug money and criminal funds. There is also some evidence that the CIA helped to fund the Afghan mujahideen in their war against the Soviet Union in the 1980s using this bank. On July 5, 1991, a court in Luxembourg ordered the Bank of Credit and Commerce International to close its doors since it was so fraught with problems and was "hopelessly insolvent." BCCI paid the largest fines and forfeitures ever obtained by federal prosecutors. They paid $10 million in fines and lost all $550 million of their American assets. Later, in 2012, HSBC would top that record fine at $1.92 billion.

Can you imagine being so rich that you have to spend $1,000 a week on rubber bands to bundle your cash? Pablo Escobar's net worth was estimated to be $9 billion—all drug money. Eighty percent of the world's cocaine trade was controlled by his cartel. Now *that* is a lot of money to launder, and he did so in part through traditional laundering techniques and in part by bribing bankers.

Did you ever wonder how Imelda Marcos could own over twenty-five hundred pairs of shoes? Her husband had to support her shoe habit by laundering billions of dollars of stolen public money through US and Swiss banks. The number one most corrupt leader on the top ten list was the Indonesian president Suharto, who was forced to resign after he was suspected of laundering about $73 billion. He died before his trial at the age of eighty-six. After all of this laundering, how do these individuals end up coming to justice? Money laundering is a crime and usually carries stiff penalties and extensive prison time.

There are many monitoring tools, laws, and agencies in place to prevent and punish launderers. Financial institutions are the soldiers on the front line when it comes to the battle of money laundering. First, banks are required to watch suspicious activities such as unusually large deposits or an unexpected change in a customer's banking habits.

For instance, a patron might regularly deposit between $12,000 to $15,000 a month but then suddenly deposit a sum in excess of $100,000. If he hasn't won the lottery, this should be considered unusual.

A Suspicious Activity Report (SAR) is one of the tools provided by the Bank Secrecy Act (BSA). This report is required to be filed for any transaction that is deemed "out of the ordinary." If a SAR is not filed, the bank or the employee could be punished or fined. In compliance with the Money Laundering Regulations Act of 1993, banks must train applicable employees on procedures for recognition and reporting suspicions of money laundering, and they are required to employ a "Money Laundering Reporting Officer." If a bank employee is convicted of failure to report a suspicion dealing with drug trafficking or terrorism, they can be fined or imprisoned up to five years, or both.

Imagine my surprise.

THE CUBICLE OF DEATH

One afternoon, I was sitting in my cubicle, having a temporary crisis of faith, wondering if anything I was doing would matter. I picked up the phone and called my dad at work to say hello. No answer. I called home, and my mom picked up the phone. She was crying. My dad had been diagnosed with cancer.

That was the moment. I was done with gathering evidence. Life was too short. I needed to go home. I got up out of my cubical and looked at the sea of debt collectors now clearing alerts. HSBC had fired hundreds of credit card debt collectors and then rehired them as Anti-Money Laundering Compliance Officers. All the folded cubicles were now erected into a sea of tiny boxes. The former department store in the strip mall was now a bullpen full of clones click-ing their mouses, allowing wire trans-fers to terrorists, resulting in sending American soldiers to their graves.

I stormed into the boardroom. The room fell silent. I said, "I am taking a leave of absence. I am not quitting. I am taking a leave. Have a good day."

It was simple and sweet. I did not quit. Not yet. I took the framed success poem my dad gave me, along with the Bible from my desk, and left everything else. Was I a disgruntled employee? Yes. I was disgruntled by my second week working at HSBC. I was disgruntled because HSBC was financing terrorism. As an American, I was mad, and I had a moral and civic duty to try to stop them.

When I took my leave of absence, HSBC had no idea that I was passing information to the CIA or that I went to the FBI with all their documents and transactions. They were soon going to find out.

A POOL OF TEARS

There was no escaping the smell of burnt wood, ash, and absolute loss. I remember, at ten years of age, standing on the black, freshly paved driveway, choking on smoke as I stared at my feet. I thought I was so cool with my Jordan Air Pumps, which were supposed to take my basketball skills, or lack thereof, to another level. The shoes—white, pure, and unused—were now never going to be put into operational status. I kept staring at those shoes with my head down. Eventually, I got the courage to look up and see the work of Providence.

My house on 115 Warren Drive had been hit by lightning at 10:42 a.m. the previous day. The lightning hit right above the bedroom I shared with my brother, blowing a massive hole through the roof and igniting a searing fire, both on the rooftop of our home and through the electrical system. A flash of light and a loud boom of thunder, and then the house began to burn. Everything gone.

I thought that this was a punishment from God. Maybe if I were nicer to my brother or a better son this would not have happened to my family. I truly believed that I was a bad person, and I took full responsibility for the fire. I know logically it does not make sense for someone to establish that deep-rooted anchor and association between a lightning strike and the kind of person I was, but for some reason, my young brain made the connection, and it stuck. As I stood firm on that black asphalt driveway, my guilt was unbearable. Out of the corner of my eye, I saw my dad, staring at what was left of our family home. My heart sank.

Dad was a diehard doctor. He was and always will be my hero. All he did was medicine and family, nothing else. He sacrificed everything for his patients and us. As he stood there looking at the ashes, his eyes had no tears. There was no anger in his face as he looked up at the still stormy sky. There was only a little smile through his bright red beard.

I always thought my dad had lost his mind, that this was a breaking point. It was not until years later, after I myself had lost everything, that I found out what that smile was.

INERTIA IS CHANGED BY FORCE

We, as adults, are sculpted by our past, no matter how long ago it was. Certain life experiences can often push us in one direction or another. The trick is to allow each lesson to become the next rung on the ladder, an essential step toward success.

As a kid, I was alone. My dad was always at the hospital, my mom was a social worker, and I spent the day at school, being tortured because of my buckteeth and stutter. One day in English class, we were assigned to read the book *Johnny Tremain* out loud.

I was in deep shit.

"J-j-johnny T-t-t-tremain..." And on it went.

I remember hearing one of my bullies yell out, "Rabbit Loser!" I was a laughingstock. After that, the main emotions I became familiar with were those of rejection. For a very long time, I was not a happy kid, and I had no prospect of becoming one.

Salvation finally came when my dad took a job as a government doctor in Florida. I got to change schools and get a fresh start. My next move needed to be strategic. I followed a plan. All through eighth grade, I kept my mouth shut—literally. I kept a very low profile to avoid anyone noticing my weaknesses. I was hiding, unwilling to take the risk of failure. I ran from confrontation, secretly wishing I were brave enough to step up and fight the good fight. That day finally came, thanks to my history teacher Mrs. Brown.

As Black History Month approached, Mrs. Brown announced auditions for a presentation. The student selected would give the Martin Luther King Jr. speech in front of the entire school—the mere thought of which terrified me.

Mrs. Brown pulled me aside after class and asked me to give it a try. I'm sure she recognized the sheer panic in my eyes, but she was relentless. She pulled out the speech and had me read it out loud. Not surprisingly, it was a cacophony of stuttering. She then gave me the best advice I have ever gotten in my entire life—words that shaped my political career and allowed me to become a strong public speaker.

"Everett, stop reading!"

"I'm sorry, I can't read out loud."

"Everett, do you believe in what Mr. King is saying?"

I nodded. "Absolutely."

"Imagine you're Martin Luther King Jr., standing in front of thousands of people, giving this speech. He's not *reading*. He is *speaking* from the heart. He is being sincere. Stop reading. Sear it onto your heart and then let the words come out. When you give a speech, it should come from within."

For weeks, I spent hours upon hours memorizing that speech. When the auditions came, I absolutely killed it.

Not one stutter.

I did not come anywhere close to the level of Martin Luther King Jr., but for the first time in my life, I could give a speech. Even my "rabbit teeth" didn't hold me back. Lesson learned. Hard work pays off. I was chosen. And on D-Day, I stood in front of the entire school in my best suit, with confidence, and spoke with absolute passion and sincerity. I got a standing ovation. It was the best day of my life.

I went home a winner, not knowing what was to come. I couldn't have imagined some of the darkest days of my life were ahead of me, but because of Mrs. Brown, I had learned to emerge from the abyss with unbridled passion and confidence. It was a simple childhood lesson that would later save my life. I will never forget what she did for me.

FINDING THE WHY

W hen you really hit rock bottom—as I have several times in my life—your core self will emerge from its depths, and you will see who you really are. You will look in the mirror and ask, "Why am I here?" And if you don't have an answer, the *nothing* will win. Finding your purpose becomes essential to your survival, and finding true friends is crucial.

My father found purpose as a radiologist, and I figured I'd gain some approval if I followed in his footsteps. Up until my senior year of high school, I thought to become a trauma surgeon, which sounded much more exciting. My father was happy with a quiet, predictable existence. Not me. My dream was to go to Yale. I was on track for that. My grades were awesome, my buckteeth were fixed. I destroyed people on debate team, and I became class president.

As usual, my goal was to make an impact. At my high school, that meant toilet seat covers for the bathrooms. I wish I were kidding. That was my platform. I was not sure how I was going to get toilet seat covers, as I had no real power as a high school class president, but something had to be done.

High school was a crazy scene. There were some real animals that went there. I remember walking into the main hallway bathroom and seeing this senior defecating in the bathroom sink. It was unreal. Who would even think to do that? I guess this particular student had some major issue with the janitor or maybe the administration. The revolt that followed his act of rebellion was a gruesome sight. I will spare you the grotesque details, but my campaign promise was a huge hit. "Toilet seat covers for all!" I ran, and I won with a landslide.

I was on the way to being an actual success. I was class president, and I finally found a good friend. My friend, Mario, was one of the best people I have ever met in my life and was truly brilliant. His future was set. He wanted to be a top lawyer and get into politics. I remember when he got into Harvard. It was a bright and sunny Florida day, and I was driving my mom's car to pick up Mario at his house so we could go to beach. I parked the gold Honda LX Civic, which I had washed and waxed the day before to impress the ladies. When I was sixteen, I thought that because the Honda Civic was a LX trim, I looked super cool driving it. I parked the car right behind Mario's dad's white truck. His dad was a construction contractor, which was a very good business to be in, as the Florida real estate market was booming in 2000. I got out of the car, weighing a solid one hundred twenty pounds, wearing the GAP and Old Navy shorts and shirt my mom had picked out for me. I walked up to the door. The day was going to be awesome. I even had on my cool clip-on sunglasses from Walgreens. I rang the doorbell and there was a faint bell sound from within the house. The doorknob turned and Mario's dad answered. His sullen face hung in front of me, almost colorless. I remember asking him if Mario was "ready to rock." I remember his words echoing in my head. I remember the gasp of coldness as I breathed in the *nothing*. Mario was dead.

I was sixteen years old when two kids doing drugs killed Mario in a car accident. It was just about three weeks after he was accepted to Harvard. How does one process the unthinkable? I asked myself a very dangerous and old question: *Why wasn't it me?*

Days later, I stood in front of my friend, laid out in the casket, his lifeless face with makeup on it and little sutures sewn in, holding the gashes together. Mario's eyes were closed, his arms crossed over his chest. They dressed him in his nicest suit.

The room emptied, and I just stood there right in front of the casket. I didn't cry. I didn't feel anger. I felt nothing. I was numb. There was no emotion. I stood in front of the deep mahogany wood coffin, staring at my friend's lifeless face. I too was dead in that moment. It felt like my soul left my body. I was devoid of light.

My dad was waiting patiently for me in the car. I do not know how long I stood there, but eventually I felt his hand on my shoulder. He said nothing. I said nothing. There was nothing left to say. My dad, my hero, could not be my Superman any longer and he knew it.

We drove home in his gray Mitsubishi Galant. I opened the door, and my mom, teary-eyed, offered comfort, but I just walked past her and went into my room, which was covered wall-to-wall with debate and science fair awards. I took off my suit jacket, struggled with my tie, got undressed, turned off the light, and climbed under the covers. No tears. No questions. No listening to my parents talk in the nearby kitchen. Just blackness. The *nothing* had taken over. In my sleep, it whispered to me.

"Own your life," it said.

I know now as an adult that the world is far from fair. I have been fighting for years to lessen the equality gap of justice. But as a kid, I thought of the world as a mathematical equation: $a + b = c$. If I did what I was supposed to—or more along the lines of what other, respected people thought I should be doing—then my actions would yield the c result, a positive outcome.

As children, we're told if we have good behavior all year, Santa would be especially rewarding. That sounded fair and, as a kid, it's all about your world being fair. My fairness fairy tale ended the second that lightning bolt hit my house. Mario's death was a far more menacing lesson in fairness: *Bad things happen to good people.* On top of that, I thought I was partially responsible for Mario's death. If only I called him and told him to come over and chill that night. If only I wasn't so selfish about going to the beach, then he wouldn't have gone out the night before to buy whatever he was buying. If only . . .

Years later, an idea recurred in my brain like a cancer: *I must be a bad person.* In 1763, Thomas Bayes—the genius probability mathematician—tried to prove the existence of God and failed, instead coming up with one of the most important theorems of all time: Bayes' theorem. This theorem describes the probability of an event based on prior knowledge of conditions that might be related to the event. I felt like my actions had led to the death of my friend. In my mind, I had become a product of the Bayes' theorem.

One day, in one of my rare waking moments, I sat in my room staring at the walls, overcome with regret, and I suddenly felt motivated to take the *nothing's* advice. It was time to own my life. I'd start by wiping out any trace of the old me.

I did not even bother putting on clothes. I walked out of my room in my tighty- whities and went to the garage. My mother was sitting at the kitchen table. As I breezed past her, I could feel her looking right through me, helplessly, realizing her son was no longer there. I opened the garage door and was blasted with the Florida heat and humidity. I grabbed a plastic bin containing my old toys and books and dumped them on the ground. Then, with the empty bin, I went back in the house. I went back into my room, gently placed the empty plastic container down, and looked around at my so-called "achievements." All those awards meant nothing. What difference did it make? Debate award? Palm Beach County Science Fair winner?

I started on the very left side of the bedroom wall.

Bang! The once coveted certificates were thrown into the bin. Each award's fate began in the same motion. The bottom of the frame was lifted off the wall, dislodging the thin metal wire in the back that was held in place by a small nail that my dad had painstakingly hammered into the wall. My room became empty and bare. I climbed back into bed and closed my eyes.

I refused to go back to school. I could not get out of bed. I slept and slept. I didn't dream. Nothing. My mom came into my room on a daily basis for weeks, throwing the covers off of me, grabbing my legs, and pulling me out of bed. I would hit the floor and get back in. She tried everything. She even poured cold water on me a few times. Her desperation was clear. But I was simply unable to function—until about three weeks later, when the numbness wore off and I began to feel again.

I was angry—at everything and everyone.

To this day, I feel horrible about being such a jerk to my brother, mother, and father. I hope they understand that it was not personal. I was angry. The anger brought on questions I could not answer, which made me angrier. It was a vicious cycle. I couldn't bear the injustice. Why is there so much evil in the world? Why did Mario have to die? Why is it that my house was hit by lighting? Why is my dad driving around in this piece of junk Mitsubishi Galant when there are bad people who are wealthy and driving Ferraris? Why are the people who killed Mario not dead? Why must some kids go to community college just because they don't come from wealthy families, while the rich kids get to go to the University of Florida? Where is the equality? Why are these deadbeat drug dealers out having a blast and getting away with killing my friend?

Each and every one of us hits rock bottom at some point in life. Hitting rock bottom isn't what you see in the movies, like being passed out on the floor with a bottle of rubbing alcohol from the drugstore just to get a small alcohol fix, as your teenage kids are being escorted out by social services. Or wearing ragged clothes and no shoes, exposing charcoal-black bare feet, which are planted on the side of an intersection while you hold a sign up to passersby that says, "No Food or Shelter." Rock bottom isn't standing in your driveway as a group of mobsters come to collect your family's cars as payment for the previous night's gambling losses.

Rock bottom is not so obvious.

It's just a feeling. You can lose every single material possession and still not get there. You can have everything in the world a person could want and achieve rock bottom status. You hit rock bottom when you lose your purpose and pure apathy takes over.

I had hit rock bottom.

Light can only be created with energy. Energy requires action. Action turns darkness into light. Those who do not take action will die at the bottom of the pit, alone and in the dark. Trust me on this. *Light the candle.*

I got out of bed and stood in front of my bathroom mirror. I still remember my young, sixteen-year-old face staring back at me as I said to myself, "Everett, you have nothing to lose."

I had rediscovered my purpose: stop injustice.

EXECUTING YOUR WHY

B *reathe, Everett. Breathe. You need to get this intelligence. This is* *for the greater good. These drugs are killing people. You need to do something about it. Dealers like this killed your best friend. Check the wire. Testing, testing . . . 1 . . . 2 . . . 3. I think it's working. I hope I am in the right place. It's possible there was a mistake. Just hang out longer. Calm down. Wait! A car is pulling in the parking lot. This has to be them. It is two in the morning on a weeknight. This has to be them.*

One thing I have always been very good at is harnessing and focusing my emotions. I wanted to take down drug dealers. Becoming a nark seemed like a rational and logical move. I wanted a sense of purpose, to fight for what is right, and the approval of people I respected.

It was maybe a month after Mario's death when I decided to go to the police. I needed to do it in secret, because if my parents found out, I would be in deep shit. I knew I was doing the right thing and it was in line with my father's moral compass, but something told me that my dad would not approve of this one.

I decided to make my move when my dad was at work and my mom had her day off. The aforementioned scenario was key because I needed to be able to take the car to school. I couldn't have my mom drop me off at the police station. After hours of my so-called high school education, I drove my mom's gold Honda Civic to the main police station in downtown West Palm. I pulled into this giant parking lot with lines of police cars in front of a militaristic-style building. In the distance, over the palm trees, I could see the county jail towering up into the sky. I smiled, imagining myself testifying against some animal—the dove flies across the courtroom, the prisoner is escorted from the building, consuming my sight. Justice served cold. Clearly, I watched too many detective movies.

As my key turned the metal locking mechanism on the car door, it hit me: I am about to walk into a police station to become an informant. The reality of the situation sunk in, and I started shaking. The car keys in my right hand began to jingle. I took a deep breath, with my left hand on the roof of the car, and looked up at the bright blue sky. I remember that there were no clouds; it was a deep sea of blue. My closed eyelids created darkness, which was all too familiar. I felt the *nothing* again. I felt the anger. I felt the vengeance. I felt my purpose. Ultimately, I felt like a kid who might be making the biggest mistake of his life.

The doors to the police station were made of blistering hot steel. The Florida heat actually made the door painful to open. I was prepared to walk into a scene from a 1980s *RoboCop* movie at a Detroit police station. Criminals would be handcuffed, led by an officer as they yelled, "Screw you, coppers!" A detective at his desk, with a phone tucked against his ear and a pad of paper in his hand, would yell across the station, "Joe, we got him! They are bringing him in now!" Then some kind of alarm would ring and all the cops would put on riot gear and start running out the door.

RoboCop, the movie, got it all wrong.

I walked into the lobby of the police station. There was a white tile floor and a locked door that required you to be buzzed in to get through. The only place I could go was up to a series of three, plate glass windows, where there was a nice, calm line of people. Each-window had about three or four people waiting in line, so I chose the window all the way to the left, as there were just three people and it looked like the person at the window was almost done. *Wrong!* My line lasted the longest, and I stood there for forty-five minutes. By the time it was my turn, all my adrenaline had drained away.

At that age, I had a limited attention span, and for a couple of minutes, I forgot what I was doing there and thought I was paying a speeding ticket. At the window was not the battle-hardened street cop I had envisioned, but a nice, sweet woman. I do not think she was even a police officer. Maybe she was a clerk or office worker or something. She asked me through a microphone, "How can I help you?"

Now, I was stuck between a rock and a glass wall. There was a line of people behind me, and I was being asked what I wanted in front of other people by someone who possibly was not a cop behind a plate glass window. I had stood in line for forty-five minutes and still never considered this scenario. What the hell was I supposed to say in front of group of people from God knows what background?

I imagined myself saying, "I am Everett Stern, and I want to sell drugs for the police and then snitch on the drug dealers, resulting in their prosecution." But instead, I stuttered through a mess of *uh*s and *um*s. I thought this sweet old lady was going to hit a red button, alerting the whole police department to come arrest me. Luckily, I thought of something.

"Ma'am, may I please speak to a police officer?"

"What would you like to talk to an officer about?"

"Uh . . . It's personal, ma'am. My apologies. I just need to speak with an officer in private."

Finally relenting, she said, "Please wait by the secured doors, and an officer will come meet you."

As I stood by the secured door, I started to panic. My fantasy was becoming a reality, and I got really scared. I never had much interaction with the police before, except for how nice they were to me when I was a little kid and my brother and I wanted to see what happened when we called 911. But I digress.

Buzz. The secured door opened. A police officer walked through. Right off the bat, he did not seem too happy with me; I was automatically a bother. This was not the police officer's fault, as he had no idea why I was there or what I wanted to do. I figured he'd warm up when he heard I wanted to step up to the plate.

"What do you want?"

"Is there a place we can talk in private? There are a lot of people here."

"No. Here is good. How can I help you?"

"I want to work for the police."

"You have to have graduated from high school and the academy. Did you graduate high school?"

"No, sir. I'm sixteen."

"You have a way to go. Just stay out of trouble and do well in school."

"Sir, I am class president and I have good grades. I want to help now. I want to help your drug department."

"You want to be a CI?"

My face went blank. "What's a CI?"

"Confidential Informant."

That was it. There was a name for what I wanted to do. The door was open, and I wanted to walk right through it. I would get justice for Mario, make my parents proud, and make a difference.

But he continued. "CIs have to be seventeen unless they have their parents' permission."

"I talked to my parents, and I have their permission." That was a lie.

"Kid, trust me on this, go back to school and become a police officer. Then go after drug dealers."

"Sir, with all due respect, I want to do this now." I said it with complete conviction. He saw in my eyes that I wasn't going to change my mind. I felt in my heart I was doing the right thing.

"Okay, kid. Write down your name and number, and I will talk to the narcotics guys," he said reluctantly.

"Yes, sir. Thank you very much for the opportunity."

When they finally called, I was prepared to go undercover. Unfortunately for me, they had no interest in taking that kind of risk with a sixteen-year-old kid. They wanted me to simply keep my ear to the ground and provide information whenever I had it. My disappointment was evident. I wanted more. So, I decided to go rogue.

I made friends with one of the dealers at my school—a druggie, well on his way into a downward spiral. I kept thinking of Mario, how a kid like this dealer was the reason I had lost my friend. It kept me motivated. He was the typical wigger. Harmless enough, but the drugs were getting to him. I could see it in his face. He was so white and sick looking and had red, bloodshot eyes. I will never forget those eyes. They were dead. The *nothing* had taken over. I ran into him in the food court and after some small talk, he asked me if I wanted to party with him sometime. I knew exactly what he meant, and I said yes. I asked if he had good shit.

"Stern, the best eight ball you will ever have," he said. And we made plans to meet.

Before I knew it, I was face-to-face with him in a parking lot at two in the morning. When he got out of his broken-down, white Cadillac and approached me, I noticed his face was as white as a ghost. He had a thick head of black hair that was topped with a sideways baseball cap. I had a wire taped to my chest and the recorder in my pocket. It was the summer of 2000, and Bluetooth did not exist; I was relying on an old-school micro recorder. Digital recorders were soon to replace the micro cassette tape, but for this operation, I had to rely on what I had at hand. I thought about bailing. Too much could go wrong here. The asshole drug dealer waiting in the Cadillac for this stupid kid, who I was pretending was my friend, could have a gun and freaking shoot me. What I was doing in that parking lot was very stupid and dangerous. I was specifically told by the head of narcotics not to go out on my own. His exact words had been, "Listen to me very carefully, kid. Do not do anything without us present or without approval."

Did I listen? Obviously not. I felt the risk was justified. My friend was dead, and I wanted every one of these drug dealers in jail. This was payback.

"Sup, man? Do you have the money?" he asked, twitching.

"Yes."

"Let's get this party started! Hop in the back, and we will hook you up."

The Cadillac was old, but it did have comfortable leather seats. I can still remember the feeling of sinking in. I also remember the dreaded sound of my potential death, when the back door slammed shut, locking me inside with the asshole.

"How much do you want?"

"An eight ball," I said, not completely sure what that meant.

"Do you want to try it? This is good stuff."

Damn, I thought to myself. *You do not do drugs. You cannot try this shit. If you refuse, then they will know you are a nark. The recording is running. What do I do?*

"Taste it." He opened a cellophane bag, and I dipped my finger in, coating the tip of it with fine, white powder. He looked down to tie the bag, and I quickly wiped my index finger on the inside of my thumb getting rid of the powder before putting it in my mouth.

"That is some good shit. How much?" I said, feeling like I was playing the role pretty well.

"Fifty bucks."

This son of a bitch is ripping me off! I put my anger aside at the monetary injustice and gave him the money. I just wanted out of this car. My "friend" was in the front seat, already sniffing away.

"Here is my number. If you need more, I can work with you on price," the asshole said. Well, at least the drug dealer was somewhat reasonable.

I opened the door and got out of the car, praying to God the tape recorder didn't fall out or make a noise. I ended up making it out safely and stood in the middle of the parking lot as I watched the white Cadillac back out and drive away. *I did it!* I was ecstatic. A deep-seated void and vicious wound felt healed. I beat the *nothing*. I lit the candle and turned darkness to light. Now that the room was illuminated, I could see again—and I could see that I was in deep trouble.

I'd broken a number of rules. I needed to have police presence there, but they were not. I was not technically a confidential informant; I was just someone "helping the police" by buying drugs.

All I needed to do was get the intel to the police immediately and report the tags so they could be found. I had one small problem, though: I had a bag of cocaine in the left pocket of my dark-navy jeans. Okay, maybe not a small problem. This was a *big problem*. I did not care that I was not allowed to conduct a "drug deal" on my own. I did not care that I myself was committing a crime, as it was for the greater good. I tossed the eight ball in a nearby trashcan and headed for the nearest police cruiser I could find.

"Are you an idiot? Shit," he mumbled. I think I ruined his night. I handed over the tape, gave him the car's license plate number, and didn't mention the eight ball. "Kid, you're going to get yourself killed. If the car is in the area, they could drive by here and see you talking to me. Put your hands behind your back."

"Why?" At that, I panicked. I was getting arrested. *I did the right thing, and I'm getting arrested!* I will never forget the cold steel being enclosed around my wrists and then three clicks as the cuffs were tightened and locked.

The cop opened the back of his patrol car and said, "Watch your head."

It was my first time in the back of a police car. The seats were a blue plastic, the back windows had bars on them, and there was a giant, plate glass divider in between the back and front seats. I started to cry. Only thirty minutes ago, I was the champion of justice—and now I was handcuffed in the back of the cruiser on the way to jail, crying with my head down and thinking about how my mom was going to have to pick up the Civic at the police impound. Then I heard the crackling of sticks and gravel. I looked up and saw through the police car windshield that we were not at the police station but in a park. The cop got out and opened my door. I heard the police chatter of codes coming from his radio. He pulled me out of the car and faced me in the direction of where the headlights were pointing into the park. The only light came from the headlights of the car.

"I am not taking you to jail. I took you here to make sure the dealers did not see you interact with me—and to scare the shit out of you so you do not do this again. Stop now, kid. Promise me."

I made my way to my mom's Honda Civic and drove home.

The next day, I woke up at around noon. I was exhausted from the night before, but I was a new man. Before I got out of bed, I lay tucked under my covers with a nice smile for a good two or three minutes. I showered, dressed, and felt a full two inches taller. My family was having lunch, and the whole family was talking and laughing. I knew I righted a major wrong in this world. I sat down at the kitchen table in between my brother and my dad. My mom was directly across from me. My dad always believed in a round table for equality, like the knights of King Arthur.

My mom offered me a turkey sandwich and coleslaw. I was starving from serving the cold cuts of justice. My dad asked me about my date the night before.

"How was the date? Did you have fun?"

"It was awesome. We went to go see *Gladiator*. Amazing movie. You have to see it, Dad."

"What is her name again?"

"Hannah."

"Was Hannah out buying drugs also?"

My mother was in the process of bringing the turkey sandwich over to the table when she dropped the whole thing on the floor. Luckily, it was a paper plate.

The round, King Arthur's table was not the table of equality anymore. The kindest and gentlest person I have ever known beat the shit out of me that day. And, in retrospect, I can't blame him.

That day I learned—after conducting a mini-intelligence operation for the greater good, only to get whipped—that right and wrong is subjective. But despite my parents' disapproval, I continued to gather intelligence on drug dealers all throughout high school. If you are reading this book and sold me drugs in high school—yes, I was spying on you. Sorry.

THROWN INTO THE PIT

A recurring theme throughout my life has been witnessing flawed social contracts, breaking them, and then trying to mend them. But at the age of sixteen, this theme really reached a peak. The police narcotics detective assisted me in gathering intelligence, but he seriously underestimated my motivation and lack of self-preservation.

The anti-narcotics efforts were not fun; they cost me friends and time I would have otherwise spent just being a kid. Were my actions on the nutty side? Yes. But the nutcases in this world get things done. Did my efforts curb the sale of drugs and save the day? No. But I learned critical intelligence gathering skills. Years later, when I was sitting in a hotel room with the CIA, those skills were highly admired. You can't make an omelet without breaking some eggs, and at least I tried to make an omelet that nourished the community in which I lived. I was not confused after the narcotic detective's harsh words for me, or by the beating administered by my dad. There was zero confusion. I knew I was right.

Still, I stopped the drug dealing surveillance when I

graduated high school. I knew I had to get out. Not just because of the danger posed by drug dealers, but because I had the burning desire to go out on my own. I was seventeen years old in May of 2002. I was already accepted into Franklin & Marshall College, and I did not want to spend my summer waiting tables. I wanted to experience something new and exciting. I remembered that I had a distant cousin who worked on Wall Street, but I wasn't sure what he did. I didn't even know what firm he worked for. I called my grandparents and asked for my cousin's number. I called my cousin, and after five minutes of catching up, I asked him if he was hiring any interns. He said if I wanted to come work on Wall Street that I should come up and they would find a spot for me. There was only one catch: there was no pay.

Despite that fact, I was so excited to have an internship that I innocently forgot to ask for the specifics. Looking back, it's clear I simply wanted to regain my parents' approval. The internship could replace all those awards I ripped off my wall and threw into a plastic bin. The internship represented getting back what I lost at a time where loss should not even be a factor. Before I left for New York, I was extremely nervous that I might fail or be fired. I was almost eighteen years old, with zero finance experience—or any experience at all, for that matter. Yes, the anxiety was clear and present.

It was time for me to walk through the doors of the American Stock Exchange. There were two entrances in the front that were heavily guarded. One said *Members* and the other entrance said nothing. It was just a couple of doors. I chose *Members*. This entrance had a series of metal barriers that led the line of people inside the exchange—very similar to how cattle are led from one barn house to another. Most of the people I was in line with were wearing blue jackets with a white stripe down both arms. The white stipe was a mesh material with holes. There were tons of security and heavily armed police. The American and New York Stock Exchanges were tier-one targets for terrorists. I walked in between the metal barricades, where there were tons of tourists taking pictures. A security guard and a policeman stopped me as I approached the security checkpoint.

"Kid, you can't go in."

"This is my first day. I'm an intern."

"I don't care if it is your birthday. You are not getting in. First off, this is a *Members Only* entrance and you are not a member."

The security guard was right. I was not a member, but I didn't understand what a member was.

"A member of what?"

I asked him to call my cousin to verify. He did. Then proceeded to tell me to get out of the line until someone came and got me. The other members I was in line with seemed to be happy with this outcome because it reinforced their status. There was a clear divide between members and nonmembers. It was like first class and coach. Members of the Stock Exchange were first class. The runners and clerks were coach class.

This young guy named Jay met me outside of the exchange and escorted me into the clerks' entrance. He didn't introduce himself or even say, "Welcome! Glad to have you."

He just said, "Move it—the bell is going to ring soon."

A bell? What bell? I thought he was talking about the bell in the Trinity Church. I never heard of a building having a bell.

I went through the metal detectors at the unmarked clerks' entrance and was completely violated by security. They gave me an all-out pat down and forced me to take multiple runs through the metal detector. It was like going through airplane security but times ten.

I walked five steps, and then I saw it. The infamous "floor." Grown men screaming at the top of their lungs, computer screens everywhere, television monitors, stock quotes, and CNBC. Then, I saw a reporter on one of the monitors, reporting from twenty feet away from me. I couldn't believe it. I made it. Then I saw a black Lab walk by with a SWAT team member holding the leash.

"Don't pet the dogs," Jay warned.

"Why are there dogs here?"

"Bombs."

I struggled to keep up with him, overwhelmed by the pace. I was on another planet. We went up an escalator to the second floor. The New York Stock Exchange has one level and the American has two. The second level is the mezzanine.

It was like a loft apartment. One of the more interesting things about the American Stock Exchange was the placement of the counters. I remember, from the movies, seeing the New York Stock Exchange, which had the circular post where traders went up to a special trader called the specialist. The specialist is the market maker or the one that tries to keep a liquid market for the stocks to which he's assigned. The specialists on the New York Stock Exchange are the ones who are stationary at the post with the clerks and interns inside. The American Stock Exchange was like being in a never-ending pharmacy. There were no posts on the Amex. The Amex had these giant, pharmacy-type counters that raised the specialists above the floor. The clerks stood next to each specialist, behind the counter. I found out that the specialists, brokers, and traders were considered members. Being a member meant you either owned a seat on the Stock Exchange or leased one from another member. Some investors would buy a seat on the exchange and lease it out to make passive income. If the market was doing well, more people would want a seat, and the price of the seat would go up.

As it turned out, I was interning for a very prestigious firm that specialized in trading and keeping liquid markets. What confused me was that the specialist was trading his own capital for profit while, at the same time, keeping an orderly market. To do this is a major conflict of interest because specialists see everything before the public does. They basically rig the system—and it's legal. During my time there, specialists were making millions of dollars a year at the Amex—same thing for the New York Stock Exchange.

Other Exchange members, such as traders and brokers, also had a major advantage over the public. They could see things the public could not, such as where crowds were forming or if another trader was going to start selling off major shares. This was why they bought the seats. I did not know any of this on my first day of the internship, but I certainly knew it on my last. My dad always preached about earning an honest dollar, but everything these members did on the Exchange was legal—and they made a fortune doing it. How does one determine if something is an honest dollar? That is not an easy question to answer. But first, let's get back to my so-called internship.

Jay brought me up to meet my cousin, who was a specialist at the firm. He was standing behind the giant pharmacy counter, looking down at some traders and brokers, yelling at them in code. He was busy, so Jay brought me to another specialist. I will call him Dick. Before Dick could open his mouth, a mountain of a man who I'll refer to as "Muscles" started screaming at a fellow broker.

"Fuck you! You fuck me! I am going to knock your fucking teeth out!"

The second broker then charged Muscles, and both brokers got restrained and pulled away from each other as they were screaming with clenched fists. None of the specialists at my firm seemed to find this unusual. Dick didn't even bat an eye. I always thought adults were supposed to act a certain way. Teachers in high school certainly didn't act like this. None of the adults I knew acted like this—especially at work. But here on the Exchange, this was just another normal day.

Casually, Dick said, "Stay away from Muscles. He will kill you."

"Yes, sir. I read the option book, but I don't—"

"I don't give a shit about the option book. You are not here to trade options. You are here not to screw up our lunches—especially my pastrami sandwich, which you are going to get from a special deli I like in midtown. Your job is to stand here next to the specialists and learn by osmosis. Keep your mouth shut, listen, don't touch anything, stay away from Muscles over there, don't mess up our food, and do what we say. Also, I heard you came all the way up from Florida, so we will pay you $300 a week."

"Three hundred dollars a week? Thanks!"

I think Dick thought I was being sarcastic, but I was really being sincere. I'd never made $300 a week in all my life. My dad was going to be proud. I was seventeen years old and making an honest dollar. No more allowance from my parents for the rest of the summer. How wrong I was! New York City was not like Florida. Living in New York was outrageously expensive, and $300 a week barely covered my train fare and a few extras.

But even though I was way below the poverty level, I knew this internship was a big opportunity. I was happy to deliver their lunches. Just being there and learning through osmosis was a major achievement and opportunity that I am forever grateful for—despite the fact that it was a miserable experience because of the level of abuse I experienced on the floor. I was even slapped in the face by Dick. Literally bitch-slapped. I took it. I cried in the bathroom that day, but I took the abuse a Wall Street intern has to take. I wanted to complete the internship and make it. It was a rite of passage. I learned very fast that the people who have the highest-paying jobs on Wall Street got those jobs because of who they knew. I needed to get in with those people. At that point in time, I thought I wanted that kind of life.

One of the specialists was in his late twenties and making $800,000 a year. The money these guys were making was unreal. Even though Dick made my life a living hell, and even though the members fought among themselves, they were a brotherhood, and I wanted to be a part of that. I wanted to be a part of something bigger than myself. My young brain saw the money and lifestyle and wanted to be accepted by these people. My need for approval was what got me through that internship. Well, to be honest, it was my need for approval, plus partying, yachting, Asian Massage

Parlors, alcohol, and strippers. My days of the internship were horrible, but there were lots of perks at night.

My first perk actually came during the day. Dick was simply a jerk throughout the entire internship, but the other traders, brokers, and specialists took a liking to me. When they said, "Jump," I said, "How high?" I only messed up one lunch order by getting spicy mustard on the pastrami and rye sandwich instead of the classic New York deli-style Russian dressing. That cost me an extra trip to the deli and a yelling.

After a while, I developed two nicknames: "Stern" and "Easy E." I thought the "Easy E" thing was sort of a compliment until I found out I was called that because "Easy E" was a rapper who died of AIDS. Either way, I was happy to be given any kind of nickname. No matter how mean some of them could be, they still took me in. I was part of the little club, in an intern capacity. I came to believe some of the traders respected me for putting up with the hazing so well, even if I had to do push-ups every time I screwed up or didn't listen.

It wasn't completely machismo, though. The hazing had a purpose. It established a brotherhood, like a fraternity, and it got the point across that if you make a mistake on the Stock Exchange, you could lose everything. If you punch in one extra zero on a number of an order, it could bankrupt the whole firm. It was serious business, with no room for mistakes. My second week there, I stood behind the specialists' pharmacy-like counter and watched the traders in the crowd below, trying to pick up on the Wall Street lingo they were using. Then, eleven o'clock hit and the whole floor shut down. It was amazing how the entire stock market just went on ice for an hour, as traders and brokers got their lunches.

I was about to start taking lunch orders when a man named Brooks turned to me, pointed to my tie, and said, "Stern, what is that?"

It was the same tie I had been wearing since my first day. I only had one—the one my grandma bought me at Macy's.

"Stern, why are you wearing that piece of shit on this floor?"

"Sir, I don't know. My grandma gave it to me."

Before I knew it, he grabbed a pair of scissors and cut off my grandma's tie, just leaving the knot. I was devastated.

"Stern, go down to Brooks Brothers by Century 21 near the World Trade Center and buy yourself a decent tie. Come back here looking sharp." Brooks then handed me $200, which was close to my weekly pay.

"Take a cab and get back here ASAP. Just tell the cab driver to take you to Brooks Brothers by Century 21."

I'd never even heard of Brooks Brothers. When I got there, an elderly, well-dressed salesman with a tissue folded into a triangle in his suit pocket approached me. I could tell immediately he did not want me there. "Sir, can I help you?"

"I need to buy a tie."

"I can see that," he said, referring to the knot still tied around my neck. "Let me guess: you're a Wall Street intern." He gave me a sympathetic look. I guess he felt kind of bad for me.

"Yes, sir." I showed him the $200, and he led me toward the most gorgeous ties I'd ever seen. They were thick, luxurious, and expensive, but I still preferred the now shredded one my grandma bought me for thirty bucks at Macy's.

My grandma was on a fixed income and, to her, thirty dollars was a lot of money. I swallowed my anger as I sifted through the table of silk ties. I found one with deep-blue and white diagonal stripes. It oozed Wall Street. I bought the tie and had the salesman help me put it on. I was still not good at tying my own tie. I wondered how many interns he'd sold ties to since the beginning of the summer.

When I got back to the Exchange, the specialists and traders gave me a cheer. "Easy E! Looking sharp!" I felt like a new man, standing tall as I walked back toward my firm.

Then I noticed a grave danger dart out of nowhere like a great white shark. He was over six feet tall and a broker, so he had a headset on and would've looked like a mission commander in a war zone if it weren't for his blue AMEX members jacket and the white mesh stripes running down his arms. He came right up to me, face to face, and grabbed my left arm. I nearly wet my pants.

"I hear you're the new intern. The next time you go into the bathroom, I am going to fuck the living shit out of you."

He dropped me and took off to yell at another broker on the floor.

I looked back at my post. My fraternity yelled out from above me, "Stern, you had better not take a piss!"

Note to self: avoid the great, white, six foot two stockbroker from Staten Island who could easily resurface from the depths below and sodomize me in the bathroom.

Once I was back with the fraternity, they all praised me on the new tie. I offered Brooks back the change.

"Keep it, Easy E. You will need it for a tip. Let's go relax. Another intern from another firm is going to deliver the lunches today. You come with us."

Dick slipped an arm around me and asked, "Easy, have you ever been laid?"

All I could manage was a stutter.

Dick yelled back at my cousin, "You sent us an intern that hasn't been laid! This is fucking awesome!"

Weird. The guys liked me more after they found out I was a virgin. I regretted not getting laid in high school, but I was too busy dealing with dead friends and spying on drug dealers.

"Brooks, where are we going to lunch?"

"I was going to take you to this nice restaurant, but now we're going to Chinatown." I had no idea where Chinatown was, but I was about to find out.

As Brooks pushed me out the door, I asked again "Sir, are you sure you don't want me to get the lunches? I'm more than happy to do it."

"Lunch is on me today, Stern. Your job is to chill. This is Wall Street, and lunchtime is a relaxing time. Have you ever had a massage before?"

"No."

"This is a great massage place. Just go with it."

We ended up on this street called Maiden Lane. No signs. No easily identifiable doors. The small building looked old and unsafe. I was extremely nervous as we walked up the narrow stairs to the third floor. My drug dealing espionage days kicked in, and I thought it could be a trap where a brute of a broker would pop out of door number two, and then *wham-bam!* On the third level, there was only one door.

Above the door was a sign that read: *Podiatry*.

"Brooks," I said, "what is Podiatry?"

"It is a doctor of the feet."

"I thought we were going for a massage?"

"Stern, shut up and just do what I tell you to do."

Brooks pushed a little white button that made a distinct buzzing sound inside the apartment—the doctor's office or whatever it was.

The door opened, and this beautiful Asian woman answered. She was about five foot five, with pitch-black hair and an unreal body, and dressed in white pants and a white tank top. She was clearly not wearing a bra. At this point, I had no idea what the hell was going on. Why would an Asian masseuse be working at a podiatry office?

The little Asian woman recognized Brooks right away. Brooks must have gone often. We had to stand all day on the floor. There were no chairs or anything, so maybe Brooks had serious feet problems. My feet did hurt from standing all day, so I can't imagine how bad Brook's feet must have been from working on the Stock Exchange for years. I think Brooks was thirty or thirty-one years old, so he was nearing retirement. Traders burn out fast on the floor, and what I heard was that traders will endure extreme stress and then retire after seven to ten years. Brooks was a senior citizen when it came to trading. I felt bad for him. His feet must've really been damaged.

Brooks said to the woman, "This is my friend, Stern. Let's do the one-hour workup."

The little Asian woman nodded her head in sort of an unofficial bow and then softly spoke in a foreign language to a group of women in the next room, all wearing white pants and white tank tops. The apartment was lit with dim lighting and candles. I saw numerous rooms created by dividers and each room had its own door.

One of the women took Brook's hand and led him into a room. I watched the door slowly close behind them. I looked around, ready to defend myself, but instead, one of the Asian women from the pack in the next room took my hand and gently led me into the room next to Brook's. This was definitely not a podiatrist's office.

As the door closed behind us, Brooks yelled out from his room, "Stern! Take off your clothes and get on the table!" I thanked Brooks for the direction because I really had no idea what was going on. I hesitantly took my cheap suit, new Brooks Brothers tie, and all my clothes but my underwear off and got on the table. My masseuse looked at me and casually glanced downward. After an awkward moment passed, I got the message.

I took off my underwear and thought, *I am seventeen, interning on Wall Street, standing naked in a room with a beautiful woman, during my lunch break, with my boss in the next room. I am out of my league.*

She began to massage my back with some kind of oil. A massage is supposed to be relaxing, but I was far from relaxed. This was one very strange podiatry office. I seriously doubted at this point that they had a valid medical license.

"You very young. How old are you?" she asked.

Before I could even respond, Brooks yelled out, "Twenty-five!"

After another ten minutes of deep-tissue massage, I realized she had never actually worked on my feet. She whispered in my ear, "Turn over." I wasn't nervous at this point; I had full confidence in her massage skills, as she did a great job on my back.

My confidence was justified.

As Brooks and I walked back to the Stock Exchange, I turned to Brooks and said, "Fuck college. I am staying here with you guys."

Massage parlors were a regular thing for Wall Streeters. It became a ritual for me that summer. Most of the guys on the Exchange did not go to college and, after finding out that hand jobs came with the job, neither did I.

I had a very bipolar type of relationship with the Wall Streeters. Every night, I was one of the guys; but, of course, the next day, I turned back into the piece-of-garbage intern. They would say the most condescending and mean things to me from nine to five, then take me out and spend thousands on me, taking me to the best restaurants and high-end strip clubs. At night, these traders could party—which was a problem, because my grandparents' bedtime was around 7:30 p.m. I was expected to be back home by then. But the nightlife was critical to the internship.

So began the ritual.

I would wake them up by coming home late, and then my grandmother would have to pour water on me in the morning so I could make the two-hour commute downtown. I was seventeen and I felt seventy. I had no idea how these Wall Street guys did it every day.

One night, Brooks and I went to this strip club in midtown. He handed me about $500 and told me to go have fun. I had never been in a strip club before, so I didn't know what to do. All I can say is that the cash was gone in about twenty minutes. The strippers saw me holding all that money and surrounded me like vultures.

Being seventeen, I actually thought these girls *liked* me. I thought I was hot shit and there was a real connection. But I spent the $500 in twenty minutes, and then the women just went away.

I told Brooks, "They lied to me! I thought they cared."

Brooks was absolutely wasted and had three girls on him when he shared a very profound and meaningful statement: "Stern, people only want what you have."

Then he gave me another $500 and said, "Stern, go put these girls through college."

Hmm. When I thought of it that way, I felt pretty good about it. *I'm contributing to the education of needy girls. Not bad, Everett, not bad.*

One of the more creative events I've ever experienced took place in a giant apartment near Wall Street. The loft was converted into a miniature Playboy mansion. And when I say Playboy, I am not using that term lightly. These Wall Street traders went out and ordered porn stars and Playboy models to fill the place.

We put a lot of girls through college that night.

I remember walking through the apartment, making my way past all these naked women with bunny ears, people having sex, cocaine on the tables, and general debauchery. It was out of a movie, complete with top-shelf liquor. At this stage in the internship, I was used to drinking (something I never did in high school) and strippers, but the cocaine turned me off. Cocaine represented everything I hated and triggered a feeling of being out of control on a downward spiral. I began to feel very uncomfortable.

The guys took me to this party to get laid. I was still a virgin, though a highly advanced one. But the cocaine made me remember the kind of person I was before this internship started—the kind of person I was and the kind of man I wanted to become. Call me a prude, but I didn't want to lose my virginity to a porn star named Candy. Don't get me wrong, I am not a saint by any stretch of the imagination, but I wanted my life to have meaning. This party represented the lowest of the low. It was a time capsule, showing me what I would become if I followed this path. I finished out the internship having learned one of the most important lessons in life: *what I didn't want.* This was not the Everett Stern my father raised me to be. As I stood in the room, surrounded by every possible pleasure, I made my decision. I'd take a BJ from Candy and then head to college.

Years later, when I was running for US Senate, I went back to visit Dick and Brooks. I wanted them to see me, to see that I had become someone. At that point, the American Stock Exchange was long gone, due to the financial crisis of 2008. Some of the surviving traders took up offices in a building across the street.

I wish I could tell you that I was greeted as an accomplished person who earned their respect and admiration. I wish I could say that all the negative, vicious, and demeaning comments during my internship were issued in the name of shaping my character. But unfortunately, all I can tell you is that I wish that my tie rack—now filled with expensive, carefully chosen, pure silk, Ferragamo and Canali ties—had just one more addition to the collection: the green, polyester tie my grandma bought me in the 50-percent-off sale section at Macy's.

RETURNING TO INERTIA

I went to school at a small liberal arts college in Lancaster, Pennsylvania. My freshman year was in stark contrast to having paid models and Asian massage specialists servicing my every need.

Lancaster, PA, is a beautiful, small town in the middle of Amish country. The school was surrounded by farms and barns. Instead of models in tight tops and short skirts, Amish women wore their hair in a tight bun, wore dresses that showed no skin, and rode around in horse-drawn carriages as their matchmade husbands took the reins. These horse-drawn carriages literally rode on the open road and caused never-ending traffic jams—for what little traffic there was. I celebrated my eighteenth birthday while attending a college in the middle of nowhere, just weeks after leaving New York City. Dealing with this mundane existence after the "high" of the summer internship was more than a little difficult.

The absolute *blah* and static state of college hit me in the first week, when I was given an assignment to write an essay on the history of the Indians and the buffalos that grazed the Great Plains of the Midwest. No more BJs from Candy; from then on, it was buffalos and Indians.

I was given a reading assignment, which I of course did not read. I bullshitted my way through the paper and failed. I loved the professor, though. She was really into history and was a kind woman. She was so nice that she actually had mercy on me and gave me a C so I would pass the class. I still keep in touch with her to this day.

Looking back, I wish I'd studied harder and taken full advantage of the academic opportunity. At that time, I thought education was pointless, but it was actually critical. When I was older, it took tremendous self-discipline to bring myself up to speed.

Sometimes, what seems insignificant can play a major role in your life later.

The college curriculum was rigorous, but I simply didn't care—at least not about what was being taught. What did I do in college? Where did that $30,000 a year go? It went directly into my gas tank. I drove. I drove for hours. I have no idea what I thought I might find, but I suddenly decided to drive around the Unites States in search of something. I drove back and forth to New York. I drove to Washington, DC. I drove in circles. I was always driving. Ask any of my friends "What was Everett like in college?" and they will tell you "Stern? He was out driving." I would drive all throughout the night, mile after mile, in an old, gray Ford Escort.

I was shell-shocked after the internship, and college provided me the necessary time to think. My grades suffered, eventually causing me to drop out before they threw me out, but my first college experience was critical in providing me time to think. At the time, I guess I didn't know what I was doing—but later in life, I got some advice that helped me figure it out.

I was getting burned out, and a dear friend of mine—a top hedge fund manager—said to me, "Everett, you are in a very unique position. Take some time off and think about what you want to do next. Use your money to buy time."

Back in college, that is essentially what I did; I used my loan money to buy time. I needed to answer the ultimate question: What is my purpose in life? Looking back, this seems like a fairly advanced question for an eighteen-year-old to have—but considering everything I had experienced up until that point, it was clear that I was not the traditional kid. I literally was shell-shocked. As I drove through many nights, more and more questions came up. The Wall Street guys had titles, money, women, and respect. I couldn't understand *why* they were so respected. Why was it that I needed their approval? Why was I attending college in the middle of nowhere, learning about the Great Plains and grazing buffalos? What was the point? What was I supposed to do with my life? My parents wanted to see me graduate from a great school. What parent wouldn't? My dad wanted to see me at a prestigious Wall Street job. All I wanted was their approval, which was then, and still is, very conditional and most likely unattainable. As I drove, I began to realize that I was willing to do almost anything to get that approval. I thought if I were important enough, I'd have a better chance. If I were rich, if I were famous, if I could make a big enough impact on the world, then maybe they'd take me seriously. I wanted to become somebody important. But I had no idea how to make that happen. I needed advice. I needed guidance from someone who knew how to go from pure anonymity to absolute fame. But there I was in the middle of Amish country with nothing to do and no family to turn to. Then, I got an idea: *Howard Stern.*

THE KING OF ALL MEDIA AND THE YELLOW BRICK ROAD

Howard Stern is my cousin, but up to that point, I'd never met him. When I was in college, I told people we were close family members and good friends. Obviously, that was a pathetic attempt to get laid. The actual relationship is that Howard is a third or fourth cousin on my dad's side. Clearly, I did not understand this "relationship stretch." I figured a cousin is a cousin, so I called my grandfather and asked if he could call Howard for me. My grandfather literally said, "Go fuck yourself," and hung up. I should mention that my dad's father was a real prick and was the complete opposite of the caring, storytelling grandpa on my mom's side.

Plan B: I decided to call the show after hours and leave a message for Howard. I called and spoke with some guy. I told him I was Howard's cousin and wanted to meet him. Dial tone. I got hung up on—again. But if there's one thing I'm very good at, it's persistence. I attribute most of my success to not giving up. Many people have lost their battle to my persistence, which can be highly annoying. But it works every time.

I called again. Dial tone. I called again. "I will get the message to Howard." A day went by. No response. I called again. Same guy answered. "I gave the message to Gary, the producer." Dial tone. I called again immediately after he hung up.

"Stern Show."

"This is Howard's cousin, and I would like to speak to him."

"Jesus Christ, kid. I'll transfer you to Gary."

I had no idea who Gary was. I had only heard the Stern Show maybe once or twice as my dad drove me to school. All I knew was that Howard Stern was big-time and I needed to meet him.

Gary got on the phone and jumped right into it. "How are you related to Howard? He doesn't know who you are."

I explained the family dynamic that I thought was ironclad. Dial tone.

I waited another day. Then I called again to show I was not going away. I was on a mission to meet the King of All Media. I spoke to Gary again, and Gary sounded seriously annoyed. He said, "Show up at 5:30 a.m. and wait in the lobby."

Mission accomplished! Persistence. They don't teach that in Amish country!

I thought I was going to just meet Howard, simply shake his hand, and get an autograph. That's not what happened. I sat in the green room, listening to the show. Howard was talking to some woman and Gary, live on the air, about this annoying, so-called cousin calling him nonstop.

I said to myself, "Oh, no. That's me."

Then Gary escorted me from the green room to the studio. I didn't understand why it was called a green room. It wasn't green. It looked like a waiting room in a doctor's office.

I will never forget the first time I saw Howard Stern. He was a giant—at least six foot seven or something. It was unreal. Nobody in my family is that tall.

Howard sat in his giant center console, talking to a woman I couldn't see. All I saw was Howard in the center, this big, fat guy with lots of stubble who as apparently Artie Lange, and Gary, a guy with huge teeth. There was no woman. I looked around, and then I saw her—Robin. She was separated from the rest of the studio behind this glass enclosure. Then I saw this other guy with long, gray hair—Fred. He was sitting near Howard. At the time, I didn't know who these people were. Then the interview started.

I have never been ripped open so hard in my life—live, with millions listening. Howard was vicious. After a few minutes of beating me up, I think Howard realized I was not some nut but just a kid who was being persistent. It certainly doesn't sound like he took a liking to me—even now, when I listen to the old tapes or read transcripts of the interview—but an amazing thing happened once we entered commercial break. Howard stood up from the center console and walked over to me. I didn't know what was going to happen, and I was scared out of my mind.

Howard smiled, extended his hand, shook mine, and said, "How are your parents?"

Every time we went to commercial, a switch was hit, a light flashed, and he became a different person. It was like Dr. Jekyll and Mr. Hyde. He turned into the real Howard Stern, a really a nice guy.

"It was nice having you on the show. Do you want an autograph? Take care and stay in touch," he said, as I was led to the exit.

I never saw him again, but I will never forget that at nineteen years old, I got to meet the King of All Media and, more importantly, the *real* Howard Stern. It was a great experience, but it brought me no closer to understanding my family or how to make a difference in the world. If anything, I was more confused.

I went home to Amish country only to find myself back at square one. Family aside, I needed to find my purpose. After two years of being in the sticks, I knew I was going to have to drop out of the school I was attending. I didn't have the grades; I needed a 2.0. I was barely there, with a 1.9 GPA, and the upcoming grades were not looking good. What the hell was I going to do? I was going to be a college dropout with no prospects or direction. I needed to go to a place I knew had all the answers, a place that held my most cherished memories as a kid: Barnes & Noble.

My dad always preached, when I was a kid, that the only way to live a meaningful life was through reading. For the longest time, I did not understand his obsession with books. Now, as an adult, I understand why they are so important and the difference they can make. As we all know, the world is not fair—especially the world of education. The child attending an inner-city school is likely to encounter a lower-quality educational system than the child attending a private boarding school. There are equalizers, though—and I do not mean affirmative action. The two great equalizers are time and books. Every person on the planet is given the same twenty-four hours in a day, and every American at least is given access to a public library. It must be instilled in children, especially those of lower economic status, that the key to success is self-education. The greatest minds throughout history were self-taught through experimentation and reading. On a regular basis, my dad would take me to Barnes & Noble to get whatever book I wanted, and I'd read with him. These are among my most cherished memories as a kid, and I always think of my dad when I browse around a bookstore. My dad taught me that learning is a lifelong process, to push the boundaries, and question everything. I questioned the source of the material. I questioned the educational material being provided. Sometimes, I even questioned the question. Then, I read every book I could find until I finally had the answer.

I fully admit that I've had to work a little harder than most academically. I'm a horrible test taker, and I have failed test after test throughout my formal education. My transcripts are littered with quite a few undesirable letters of the alphabet. But I never cared because my dad always said, "The objective is to learn, not necessarily earn the highest grade."

In school, I read about what interested me. My grades didn't suffer because I was out partying. In fact, I was usually in the library on Friday and Saturday nights. I was studying what I wanted. The ability to take initiative and control your own education is critical. The degrees and letters next to your name are important for getting jobs and making it in society, but knowing how to self-educate creates a lifelong learning process that will allow for adaptation in any environment. A key factor in battling the *nothing* and never becoming apathetic is opening a book and always asking, "Why?"

It was the first semester of my junior year—and my last semester at a school. I had come to both love and regret having to deal with life-changing questions at the expense of earning their diploma. I remember it being very cold, and there was snow on the ground. The trees were bare, and the sky was gray. Just like my mind, things looked bleak. I now had a gold, '95 Saturn that my dad bought me for $5,000. The roads were mostly clear of ice, but there were still some patches to avoid. I carefully made my way to Barnes & Noble and parked at one of the many empty spots available. Not many people were driving that day. I walked up and down the aisles, hoping to find the key, the answer, the book that would open my mind and give me a new perspective. I eventually came to the self-help section. I had no idea what I was looking for. I was browsing the outside of the book bridge. Then, I saw it. I don't know why it caught my eye, but bells went off in my head. *Awaken the Giant Within*. That was what I needed. I have never had a title of a book jump out at me like that before. I took it off the bookshelf. It was the second shelf from the top. The book was by Tony Robbins. I had no clue who Tony Robbins was. I'd never heard of him until that moment. I did not even browse the book—I just *had* to read it. There are certain moments in life where there seems to be a kind of gravitational pull that makes you do something. There was no basis or background for me to buy this book. I'd never been given direction to buy it, but I did.

I went home, started reading, and couldn't stop. I am not pitching Tony Robbins, but the book honestly provided a guide and resource for answering my deeply rooted questions. The book did not give advice; it was written in a way where I could figure things out for myself. It provided structure for my thoughts and questions to be answered. Three days later, I figured out the message in my core.

When we can't change the outcome of a painful situation, sometimes all we have left is the search for justice.

CIA RECRUITMENT

It was by far the longest drive in my life. It was only from West Palm Beach to Miami, but I was beyond nervous, and it felt like I'd traveled for days. I was dressed in my best suit—sclassic navy blue with a red tie. I sported a fresh haircut and a clean shave. Shined shoes, dialed in. The only problem was that I didn't know for what. I was not prepared. I had no idea what I was walking into. I was told my interview would be at a hotel in Miami. I needed to be there by 9 a.m. I was told that this was going to be an all-day affair.

I couldn't sleep the night before. I wanted to be a spy so bad, and I didn't want to mess up this interview. I wasn't scared to meet with the CIA, but I was nervous that I would say something wrong and flush my life down the toilet. I wanted a life of excitement, intrigue, and most importantly, I wanted to be able to look myself in the mirror and know that I was making a difference. I was drawn to the CIA over the FBI because the CIA served in silence and without any credit. They did whatever it took to protect the United States, and they sacrificed everything.

The way I pictured being a CIA officer was no family, isolation, and constant nervousness. The CIA did not appear to be a job. From what I understood from the movies and spy novels, it was a way of life. I wanted a to be part of something greater than myself and risk it all. I wanted to be part of the best of the best. My dad always told me as a kid to never be the mouse hitting the pleasure pill.

I had to break out, test the boundaries, and become my best self. I was living at home with my parents in West Palm Beach, attending the worst college in America—Florida Atlantic University—when I decided to apply to the Agency. It was a fairly simple process. I went online and filled out an application. I never thought I would actually get a callback. The site said that if I did not hear from them in forty-five days, then I was not being considered. I didn't keep exact track of the days, but after about a month, I figured it was over. What was I going to do? I was going to make myself a better applicant and try again. The people who know me best know that I am persistent—persistent as hell. If you know me and are reading this book, then I am sure I have annoyed the hell out of you at one point or another over something. Nevertheless, as I've proven many times, persistence pays off.

It was time to go. Green light. Time to jump out of the plane. The sliding doors opened when they sensed my movement. I was now in the hotel—a very nice, very empty hotel. I was extremely early, two hours early to be exact. I was supposed to be at the hotel at 9 a.m., and I showed up at 7 a.m. The traffic on I-95 is notoriously horrendous, so I left super early to make sure I was on time. Now, I had a problem. I wasn't given any details about this interview. I didn't know who I was meeting or where. I was just told to go to the conference room for the cruise line. It was 7 a.m. and I figured I had better find this room. Maybe the CIA agents would be impressed I was there so early and eager. No cruise line signs, though. I went up to the only person in the lobby, which was the receptionist.

"Good morning. Where's the cruise line conference room?" I asked nervously, realizing it was my first, unofficial CIA lie.

"Take the elevator to the eighth floor and make a left. You'll see a sign," she said casually. Clearly, she had done this before.

I decided not to go up. It was way too early. The CIA probably had a profiler or shrink up there or something. I didn't want to look like a nut or a terrorist scoping out the place. I wanted to be normal for a change. So, I had breakfast. I sat there with a cup of coffee, just waiting. The time passed by relatively fast as I imagined myself sneaking into a terrorist's house in some Arab country with a 9mm handgun, dressed in all black. I would find the terrorist, reach for my gun, and a red laser beam would cast a nice dot on the back of his head. He'd have no idea I was there.

Beep, beep, beep.

My watch went off, and I snapped out of my daydream. I was back to the real world. Time to go. I paid the bill, which I remember being insane for a cup of coffee and a couple of eggs. My parents were going to ream me out when I got home and had to ask for more allowance money because of a $30 breakfast.

As I left the hotel dining room, where my wallet was pillaged for every dime, I headed toward the elevator. I kept an eye out for CIA types but wondered what CIA agents looked like. James Bond? Some guy in a tux, drinking a shaken, not stirred, martini at 8:30 a.m. in a Miami hotel lobby? Not likely. I walked into the elevator, and there was a guy about my age, dressed like me, in the corner. We made eye contact briefly and turned toward the elevator doors.

"What floor?"

"Eight, please," I responded, playing it like the cool CIA agent I felt destined to become.

"You going to the cruise line?"

I hesitated for a moment, but softly replied, "Yes."

The elevator doors closed on our smirking faces, like a scene from *Ocean's Eleven*. The intrigue had begun.

"Agent?"

"No, you?"

I shook my head.

"Do you have any idea what is going to happen?"

"Nope," I said. An awkward pause followed, until we reached our floor. The elevator doors opened.

I stepped out into the hallway first, completely prepared for a black bag to be flung over my head as soon as I hit the carpet. We both saw the cruise line sign in front of the conference room door, which was slightly ajar. My new friend gestured for me to go first.

Gee, thanks, I thought and gave the door a soft double knock before slinking into the tiny room. There was a giant screen in the front of the room, which was set up like my old high school, classroom-style seating. Really? I thought this was a job interview. What the hell was this?

In between the projector screen and the chairs were four CIA agents. I looked them up and down, a little disappointed. They looked like normal people. They weren't even in suits. The two male agents were dressed in khakis and decent shirts, and the women wore casual dresses. Basically, you would never know these people worked for the CIA.

A spy, by definition, is supposed to not look like a spy, but for some reason, I thought there would be some kind of look to them. Like how people always say, "That guy *looks* like a cop." These people didn't look like anything. I thought there'd be battle scars on their faces from hunting terrorists in Afghanistan, or a limp from some explosion in Iraq. The agents were talking with each other when I walked in, and then they all immediately stopped and came up to greet me. They were very nice and welcoming.

No bag over the head or waterboarding to be done here. These people were some of the nicest, most normal people I have ever met. My entire idea of what the CIA was began to change. The cloak-and-dagger movie ideas were melting away with every sentence the CIA agents uttered.

"How was your drive?"

"Ah, eh . . . uh," I stuttered. *Damn it.*

"Don't be nervous. Relax. What is your name?"

I forced out, "Everett Stern."

"Welcome, Everett. It's great to have you here, and I think you will learn a lot today. We are going to be giving a presentation as soon as the other interviewees arrive."

"How many people are interviewing?"

"About fifteen or twenty. Take a seat and relax. Here," she said, handing me a CIA pin.

Really? I thought.

I sat down in the third row back so I could see some of the other people in front of me. I also didn't want to appear too anxious; I'd already screwed up royally by stuttering like crazy. More people flooded into the room. They all got a nice greeting, took a pin, and sat down. I noticed something very interesting as the other candidates walked in. Many of them were not wearing suits. One guy was wearing a military uniform, but the others were wearing Dockers or jeans and casual shirts—no ties. Why the hell would someone walk into an interview without a tie? Who does that?

"Welcome, everyone. It's an honor to have you here," one of the agents said confidently, before briefly introducing his associates. "You are all being considered for different positions with us—and you are all now rejected. Let me make myself crystal clear. We expect every one of you to tell a family member or friend that you applied but you were rejected. You will go back home today and tell everyone you know that you interviewed and did not make the cut. The good news is that you all already have the job if you pass the security clearance."

Let me explain what the CIA is and what makes them the best. They are the best because of one word: *diversity.*

One by one, he went around the room, asking each of us what we did for a living. Our answers were, indeed, diverse: pilot, accountant, gas station attendant, etc. We had almost nothing in common. "The enemy recruits everyone, so we have to do the same. The one thing we all have in common is that we are Americans. The CIA's mission is to gather intelligence, analyze it, and then convert it into meaningful information to help aid the president of the United States. We believe that the airspace between my cell phone and your cell phone is free airspace. If you do not feel that way, then leave the room now."

Nobody left.

The rest of the interview process is classified. But as I was leaving, I had an interesting conversation with one of the agents.

"Do you really want to be a Financial Resource Officer?"

"No, I applied for that job because I figured I would get my foot in the door and prove myself."

"Everett, what do you *really* want to do?" he said, looking me straight in the eye.

"I want to defend the United States. I want to fight and risk everything. I want to be in the field," I said, without a single stutter.

"You will have your official rejection letter for the Financial Resource Officer position within two weeks. You will be getting a call from a division of the Agency called the Clandestine Service. You will get a call in a couple of weeks along with your rejection letter."

After the phone call, I received another, second rejection letter. My dream of being a CIA agent was over. I never went to work for the Agency.

MY GIANT HEAD AND MEETING THE MICE

I n May of 2010, I was sitting on a metal fold-out chair, along with hundreds of my fellow students. I was wearing a mortarboard hat with a gold tassel hanging down on the right side of my face. I couldn't remember if the gold tassel was supposed to hang to the left or right, but I it didn't matter because I'd made it. I'd made it to this momentous point in my life.

The bleachers in the gym were filled with excited parents. My dad was somewhere in the crowd, but I couldn't see him. I kept looking for his once red, now gray beard to distinguish itself from the other parents, but it didn't. My row of students was instructed to stand and form a line next to the stage. We were called up name by name, and student by student climbed the stairs to receive their diploma.

I was next. The dean of the business school leaned into the microphone, which was attached to a podium set high above the graduates.

"Everett Stern, MBA," he called.

I was ecstatic. There was a row of professors on the stage, each with their hand out to congratulate me before I got to receive the coveted parchment paper. This was it. I spent years in school, having to deal with asshole professors, and now I was free to finally show how I really felt. A professor reached out his hand to congratulate me, and I callously looked at him with disdain and rejected his handshake. He just stood on the stage with his hand extended, but I promise you, no hand was given in return. I went right for what I came there for: the Master's in Business Administration diploma. I basically snatched the diploma out of the dean's hand, and as I walked off the stage, I held the diploma high in the air and yelled at the top of my lungs, "I love you, Dad!" The room busted out laughing. It was not a stunt, though. My master's degree was for the approval of my father, and even though I couldn't see him in the crowd, I had to make sure we connected as father and son at the exact moment that I received my master's degree.

Graduating from business school was only the first in a long list of steps. Next came the job hunt. I was ready, but there were no jobs available. The financial crisis of 2008 was still in full force, and companies were laying people off like crazy. It was downsizing time. Even the American Stock Exchange closed its doors. With trillions of US economic dollars gone, the highflying traders were now highflying pizza delivery boys.

I sat in my apartment during the summer of 2010, applying and applying for jobs. After a month of nonstop submissions, I realized that an MBA was not worth what I thought it was. I thought I was going to have companies calling me out of the blue to recruit me now that I had MBA next to my name, but those three letters actually hurt me in the post-2008 job market. An MBA signaled to a recruiter that I needed to be paid *more*. On a personal note, getting an MBA was critical in my long-term success because it gave me an added layer of credibility. I am not discouraging anyone from pursuing an advanced degree—just get the advanced degree for *you* and not your employer.

To be perfectly honest, I didn't learn anything in business school. In fact, I probably lost a few IQ points. The MBA did give

DARK MONEY AND PRIVATE SPIES

me credibility, though, which is important. An advanced degree opens doors later on. It is a long-term investment. I know plenty of people who are much smarter than me who dropped out of college and didn't go back. However, in our society, the letters next to your name will determine your social status to a large degree.

My advice for anyone in school is to get the best grades you can, achieve the highest level of education possible, and then forget everything you learned in school. The second you enter the real world, the academic theories don't apply. Earning a degree comes with ego, and you must strip yourself of that ego to be successful. If you think you know everything, you will not allow yourself to learn new things.

Please, make no mistake: education is key. It teaches you how to do things you don't want to do, which then gives you initial credibility. But never think that because you have a degree you know it all. I am very thankful that I recognized my business school program was underwhelming and understood my sole objective from the start: to say, "How high?" when told to jump—and then get the hell out of there.

My student loan money was running out, and I did not want to have to go back to my parents for money. That was the *last* phone call I wanted to make. I was twenty-five years old and about to run into serious financial trouble when I saw a job posting for an Anti-Money Laundering Compliance Officer position at a bank. I had no idea what anti-money laundering was, let alone what it meant to be a compliance officer, but it sounded official enough for me. I applied for the job without giving it a second thought, as I was literally applying for everything under the sun.

Actually, my approach for applying for jobs was exactly the strategy I used for dating. Ask every girl out. Dating was a numbers game—pure statistics. The more girls I approached to dance at a club increased the odds of one saying yes. I did not screen the jobs I was applying for, as they were few and far between. When

I applied to HSBC, I didn't even know it was bank; I'd never even heard of it. It could have been a local laundromat, for all I knew.

Immediately after applying, I got the call.

The HR rep's first question was, "We see you are located in Florida. Are you willing to move to Delaware?"

I faltered, not because of the location—I didn't care where I went—but because I had applied for so many jobs that I didn't know which one we were talking about. I made the quick decision to wing it.

"Of course."

"HSBC Bank is hiring for an immediate opening. When is the soonest you can come up for an interview?"

"I can fly up next week."

"We can't pay you airfare."

"No problem."

I went back to my computer and looked up HSBC. I read that it was the Hong Kong Banking Corporation, one of the world's largest banks. My interview was in New Castle, Delaware. I had driven through Delaware while traveling to my Wall Street internship back when I was seventeen. I remembered it being a tiny state because my drive through it was so short. Then I looked up New Castle, Delaware. It was in the middle of nowhere. I saw on Google that all the major banks had offices in Wilmington—the banking capital of Delaware.

I was excited, but something was bothering me. I asked myself why the largest bank in the world would be so anxious to get me in for an interview? Why was this official, anti- money laundering position being advertised on CareerBuilder, hiding the HSBC name? Why was the interview in New Castle, Delaware, far from where the other banks were operating? Each question was like a flash of light—a split second and then it was gone, discarded as my own insecurity. I soon forgot my concerns and immediately called my parents, who were thrilled for me and offered to pay for my airfare.

I flew up to Delaware from Florida the next week. I took a cab from Philadelphia International down to New Castle, which was a fortune. I did not realize the distance. I sat in the cab looking out the window, passing all the big buildings in Wilmington, where all the banks were. One more flash of light. *Why New Castle?* The driver pulled into a one-story shopping mall and stopped the cab.

"Here you go," he said, suggesting we had reached my destination.

"No, sir. I am going to HSBC Bank," I said, confused.

"This is HSBC Bank."

"This is a shopping mall."

"Used to be."

I got out of the cab and approached the front entrance. There were people in the parking lot, smoking and standing around, wearing headphones and blue jeans. A major flash of light hit me: *What the hell is this? These people are not bankers.* I remembered my experience at Wall Street and thought, *This can't be a bank. Dick and Brooks would never allow this.* Headphones? Not earbuds. Big, black headphones that you wear around your whole head. The "bankers" were basically dancing in the parking lot. I saw a little sign on top of the converted shopping mall doors—which once probably led to a food court—that read: HSBC. I was confused and felt very out of place. I opened the doors, and there was this little security post off to the right. The security guard looked like he came with the old shopping mall. He must have been transferred from mall security to HSBC guard. The guy was extremely fat, and I could hear his every breath.

"Sign in on the clipboard," he wheezed. I signed in. "Who are you here to see?"

"HR. I am here for a job interview."

"With collections?"

I had no idea what collections meant. "Compliance position."

The "mall security" managed to get off his stool, tried to pull his pants up over his stomach, and waddled to an adjacent room.

I looked around and all I could see were two hallways leading no-where—one leading straight ahead, and another to my left leading into a large room. But there was a door blocking the room, so I couldn't see what was inside.

Humpty-Dumpty waddled back to his post and pulled up his pants again before sitting down. I swear, for a minute, I thought he was going to sleep. Then the HR woman came out to greet me. She was not looking too good either.

She escorted me through the hallway to my left and then through the door, which required a key fob to open. Walking into HSBC Bank was like walking into Jabba the Hutt's lair. It was a giant room, large enough to fit at least a hundred people. The room was mostly empty except for maybe ten or fifteen people sitting in small cubicles. The rest of the room was a sea of empty and un-finished cubicles all across the floor. All of them were gray, with opaque dividers so each cubical dweller couldn't see the person to the right or left. Nobody wore suits; jeans and T-shirts all around.

Note: this was a weekday. I knew immediately that no cus-tomers were coming to this location. The walls were only half-painted. This was clearly not meant for clients. I was escorted into an interview room, where I sat down at a long table that looked like they bought it at a pawnshop. There I waited.

I was surprised when two better-dressed and intelligent-looking men walked into the room. These men weren't like the cubicle dwellers—except one of them had his sideburns cut way too high. Whatever sadistic barber this guy used had buzzed so high that it looked like he was missing a patch of hair. It was distracting, but I sensed this guy was about to become my boss.

The other guy was a former counterintelligence FBI agent. I'll refer to them as "Traitor" and "Burns." Burns was a former com-pliance officer at another bank.

The interview was brutal and mostly handled by Traitor, who was a skilled interviewer. Traitor started the interview.

"Everett, do you know what a cease-and-desist order is?"

"No, sir."

"We just got put under one, and you are part of the first wave of people to get us to comply with that order. Do you know anything about anti-money laundering?"

"No, sir. But with enough books and time, I can teach myself anything."

"Do you know what money laundering even is?"

"No, sir. But—"

"Have you ever worked for a bank before?"

"No, but I did do an internship when I was seventeen, and—"

"Do you know anyone in the compliance field?"

"No, sir."

Traitor then looked at Burns and said, "I am going to grab lunch. You take over." Traitor left the room.

Burns waited until the door shut behind him and said, "Everett, we think you are a good fit. You seem like a fast learner and a smart guy. We will give you a shot. We will email you the start date and HR will make you an offer."

"Sir, thank you so much for the opportunity! I won't let you down!"

I flew back home to Florida the next day, and that afternoon, I was made an offer to start at HSBC Bank as an Anti-Money Laundering Compliance officer in New Castle, on October 10, 2010, for $54,900.

I was blown away. I swore to God that I was going to pay Traitor and Burns back for giving me the opportunity of a lifetime by being the best Anti-Money Laundering Officer ever and getting them out of that cease-and-desist order—once I figured out what it was. I immediately went to the library and started reading every book on anti-money laundering, terrorist financing, and all relevant compliance and sanctions that pertained to banks. I was now on a mission to save HSBC Bank.

JUSTICE IS THE DEFENSE OF OUR LIBERTY—OR SO I THOUGHT

I've always hated my alarm clock. I love to sleep in. I'm more of a night person. I like staying up late into the wee hours of the morning because of the silence. There are no phone calls, fewer distractions, and a greater ability to focus. Getting up early has always been challenging for me.

After I left HSBC, my alarm clock lost its use. The 7:00 a.m. "beep" was for working people. It was a relief. Most mornings, I didn't even set it. I rose to the sun streaming in the window and eagerly spent the day drafting an intelligence report that crystalized the illegal activity of HSBC Bank—which I called, *HSBC: Sponsoring Terrorism*.

Originally, I passed information to the CIA, but once I was away from the grasp of HSBC, I could finally report to the FBI. There was no way I was going to them while I worked at HSBC. HSBC intentionally sought out former FBI agents to work in the New Castle office as "contractors." These contractors were paid close to

$100,000 a year and were used to maneuver the bank around the anti-money laundering laws. The regulators had a difficult time finding the fraud because these former FBI contractors worked miracles. My number one obstacle at HSBC was a former FBI counterintelligence agent. He was the head of the entire department, as well as the director. He was dangerous on a number of levels and would change the rules constantly.

For example, one afternoon he stood up on a cubicle desk, high above us, and announced that we could trust Saudi British Bank representatives. Therefore, any alerts from Saudi British Bank could be automatically closed. Remember, we had major backlogs of alerts and he had to find ways to get the alerts closed and out of the system. An alert had a limit of thirty days to remain open or the regulators would be alerted.

The avoidance of regulatory intervention was the catalyst for the pressure to close the alerts. Saudi British Bank was a terrorist haven and was kicking off alert after alert in the HSBC Alert Monitoring System. So, instilling trust was the only solution. He was the all-powerful wizard behind the curtain. What was worse—for me, at least—was that he was a counterintelligence FBI agent and was trained to sniff out spies. I have to say that I am proud to have gotten past him for over a year, and I think he needs to go back to the academy.

During the time I spent writing the intelligence report, I had no income, and I was living off of the $27,500 (minus the 40 percent lawyer's fee) settlement I received when the manager told me to wear a yellow star around the office. I moved from Delaware into a 400-square-foot studio apartment. It was a dump. I didn't even have a bed. I was sleeping on a camping cot that I bought at Walmart. My desk, where I wrote *HSBC: Sponsoring Terrorism*, was a plastic fold-out table meant for conventions. No TV. No radio. Basically, my apartment was not impressive. Outside of my $300, navy-blue, HSBC interview suit and my computer, I didn't own a single thing. I admit that I was extremely lonely and depressed, but writing the intelligence report kept me going. It took me about two weeks to finish writing the document that would change my life. I would write through the night, retire to my cot, and start all over again the second my eyes opened.

The day after finishing the report, I called the FBI tip line. I spoke to an operator and tried explaining the situation. I was not being taken seriously. My complaint was sucked into a black hole. My next move was to call the Philadelphia FBI field office. I spoke to a special agent who sounded as if it was his first year out of the academy and, as such, was relegated to taking inbound complaints. I tried to explain the urgency of the situation, but it fell on deaf ears.

"A special agent will get back to you, Mr. Stern."

"When?"

"I am not sure, but your complaint has been entered into our system."

I stared directly into the black hole and thought to myself, *The FBI! How are they missing the importance of this? Damn it! I am going down there.*

I set my alarm for 7:00 a.m., stripped down to my boxers, and tried to find a comfortable position on the campaign cot—which was made of metal and had one stray bar that went right into my back. I tried to stuff a pillow in between the thin mesh of the cot, my lower back, and the bar underneath. Once I found a somewhat comfortable position, I pulled the covers over me and stared through the darkness at the ceiling.

I could hear the neighbors doing their wash in the laundry room that was right across from my apartment. I could hear the quarters go into the machines, then the whoosh of the water. I listened to an entire wash cycle and remembered lying in bed like this on November 7, 2010—the night I first wrote the email to my CIA recruiter. Life changing. I had to make them listen. If there was one thing I was good at, it was persistence. I had to get the FBI to listen, because I knew HSBC was literally sponsoring terrorism and it seemed that I was unfortunately the only one willing to do something about it. I wanted justice. I prayed to God that they would listen. I prayed my intelligence did not go into a black hole. I began to drift off to sleep, listening to the water fill the washing machine for the rinse cycle.

Beep. Beep. Beep.

7:00 a.m.

I immediately popped off the cot. I went into my disgusting shower, filled with grime and whatever other shit was growing on the tiles. I put on my finest, and only, $300 navy-blue suit. I polished my Ecco black shoes with Kiwi wax to give them a nice shine and put on one of the old Brooks Brothers ties from my Wall Street days. I took five copies of the intelligence report and put them in my black, worn-out leather briefcase. I opened my studio apartment's greenish-blue door, facing the washing machine room, and slid into the cramped elevator (that should not have passed inspection).

My nerves were shot. I couldn't believe I was just going to *walk* into an FBI office.

Once I was outside, the sun was bright and the air was warm. I spotted my car parked in the second row and thanked God it was still there. One of my many concerns about where I was living was that my car would be stolen. I shoved the key into the gray Hyundai that I bought for $8,000 from a used car dealership. I opened the door and tossed my black, worn-out bag containing HSBC Bank's death sentence onto the passenger front seat. I couldn't get in.

My right hand rested on the hood, with my left hand on the open door and my body in between the driver's side door and the body of the car. Some force prevented me from getting inside. I was scared.

What if the FBI *does* listen? What if they don't throw me out? What if they take me seriously? The CIA was different. I ascertained intelligence and then gave it to them, never knowing if anything was ever done with it. The FBI I did not understand. All I knew came from movies, federal witnesses, hearings, and interviews. I was entering into the unknown. I was about to enter into a black hole—one that would rip through space and time, leaving behind a different Everett and dramatically changing the course of my life.

I remember saying to myself, "Get in the car." Eventually, I did.

I was living in a suburb of Philadelphia, so it took me about an hour, with traffic, to reach the federal building at 600 Arch Street. I parked in a garage a couple of blocks away and was not happy about the high parking fees because my cash was scarce.

As I walked up to the federal building from the parking garage, I saw the thing that melted away all of my fears and anxiety. The federal courthouse was attached to the federal building, and there was a giant engraving on the wall of the great seal of the United States, which read, "Justice is the Guardian of Liberty."

As I stood in front of the Philadelphia federal building after reading the engraving, I knew that what I was doing was the right thing. I opened one of the double doors, and there was a line of people waiting to go through metal detectors. On the inside, the federal building looked like the TSA security line at the airport, except the line was much smaller and the TSA agents were replaced with federal police officers.

As I waited in line, I saw men and women walk by to the left of the line, flashing badges and just going to the elevators. After about five or ten minutes, it was my turn. I put my briefcase on the rubber conveyer belt and watched it slide into the X-ray machine. I took out my keys and placed them in a white, plastic container that followed the briefcase. I stepped through the metal detector. Thank God, it did not go off. The federal officer then asked me for my driver's license and asked where I was going.

"The FBI, sir."

The officer handed back my ID as a second federal officer finished up going through my briefcase.

"Second bank of elevators, eighth floor."

I took my briefcase, put my driver's license back into my wallet, and thanked the officer. I followed his instructions and took the elevator to the eighth floor. The journey there felt like an eternity. I felt like I was back in the elevator during the CIA cruise line interview. Immediately upon stepping onto the eighth floor, I saw a giant Department of Justice seal. To my right, there was a memorial for all of the fallen FBI agents who served and lost their lives with the highest honor. Straight ahead of me was a bullet-proof, plate glass window, with a heavyset gentleman sitting just on the other side of the ultimate protection. I walked up to the extra thick window, spoke into the circular metal intercom, and told the guard I was here to speak with the special agent who took my complaint on the phone.

"Do you have an appointment?"

"No, sir."

"Call back and make an appointment."

"Sir, I apologize, but I need to speak to a special agent now. I have critical intelligence to provide to the FBI."

"What kind of intelligence?"

"I have evidence of HSBC Bank sponsoring terrorism. Sir, I know you are all busy, but this is a national security issue. I am not some nut coming in here. I have a full intelligence report to give to your agents. Please see if the special agent is here."

"Wait here."

A few minutes later, the special agent appeared behind the plate glass window. "I said we would call you back."

"With all due respect, there is no time for you to call me back. I have an intelligence report to give to you. This is a national security issue and involves terrorism."

"I escalated your case to other special agents. They're going to call you in when they have more information. There is already a team working on HSBC. I will let the assigned special agents know you're here."

He disappeared, and I was left standing in the lobby. I walked over to the digital memorial presentation on the television screen that showed every fallen special agent and the surrounding circumstances. I began to feel extremely depressed. I was sad seeing the pictures of honorable men and women who were killed, but I was also sad that I could still fail. *The FBI may not listen. This was a waste. I should not have come down here.* The duty officer, followed by two special agents, emerged through a security door across the room. The new special agents were wearing street clothes, but I could still see their holstered guns through their shirts.

"It is a pleasure to meet you. Thank you for coming down. We have been researching this case and I am sorry we did not call you sooner."

"It is an honor to meet you."

They reopened the security doors and brought me to an interview room. My hopes rose as they explained that there was an entire taskforce working on the case. They were ready to listen.

I handed them the intelligence report and walked them through every single detail. After the three-hour meeting, I knew the FBI took the evidence seriously. At the end of the interview, one of the special agents handed me his card with a beeper number on the back. That was the moment. There was no turning back. I was now officially a witness. They gave me strict instructions: If someone banged on my door, I was call 911 and then dial their beeper number to contact an agent, and they'd come get me. For future meetings, I could lose the Brooks Brothers tie and wear regular clothes. If I spoke to the press, I was never to mention agent names or let them use my picture. I was to avoid going public or I'd exclude myself from the witness protection program. The list went on. No turning back now.

I walked out of the federal building and once again read the words, "Justice is the Guardian of Liberty." I pulled out the agent's card and flipped it over to see the emergency beeper number. Then I looked back up at the engraving and smiled for the first time in a long, long time.

THE DUMPSTER DIVER

Shortly after interviewing with the FBI, I read a *Reuters* news article published by Cougar—the dumpster-diving reporter that plagued HSBC—but it was missing so much. I decided that going to the FBI was not enough. This reporter was hot on the trail of HSBC from the start of the cease-and-desist order. He was fixated on HSBC and was determined to expose them. He had clearly researched and published thorough stories, but he was missing one key ingredient: me.

The public needed to know that a bank here in the United States was literally financing the enemy. I decided to call *Reuters* and fill in the missing pieces.

I spoke with a receptionist at *Reuters* and was transferred to Cougar's line. He immediately answered. I explained who I was, and the next day, he took a train from NYC to Philadelphia to meet me in a hotel lobby off of Market Street. I admired him immediately. I still have the highest respect for him. When most reporters were ignoring the story, it was Cougar who pressed on.

I was invited to *Reuters* HQ and met with the entire news

team—including the Editor in Chief, who was a highly accomplished journalist. It was an honor to meet her. The *Reuters* team decided to do a new story featuring my evidence. The new story would expose HSBC and hopefully light a fire under the FBI to take HSBC down.

In the newsroom meeting, I was asked for FBI agents' names. The editor suggested the story might not run if they couldn't verify some of the evidence with the FBI. I held my ground.

"No FBI names. That is my only condition."

The story got the green light. Cougar and I met weekly and talked daily. I admit that the relationship with Cougar got a bit tense as the giant, investigative piece rolled into months of due diligence. I thought the story was going to come out right away, as I was initially told it would not take long to publish, but Cougar researched everything. He took his time. We fought on occasion, but I never lost my respect for him. Then came a moment I was hoping to avoid. I was asked to meet with the photographer. The FBI specifically told me at the first meeting not to put my photo in any news articles. A public photo could exclude me from witness protection. But the news team at *Reuters* was adamant that my photo be included in the article to give credibility to the allegations. According to Cougar, no photo and the story would be a failure.

I hung up the phone with Cougar and called my contacts at the FBI, who assured me that a photo would be like putting a target on my back. Despite the warnings, I decided that the mission was to stop HSBC Bank from sponsoring terrorism and financing the enemy. The higher purpose was to serve the United States and protect the country. The *Reuters* news article would expose HSBC and could trigger new investigations. Once the American public knew what HSBC was doing, a fire would be lit.

Just before the HSBC Senate hearings on Capitol Hill, the *Reuters* story was released with my photo. I received an email from the FBI saying, "Great job!" The FBI understood that I cared more about the greater good than my personal safety. Unfortunately, though the *Reuters* article was widely read on an international scale, the American public didn't seem to care.

FALLING INTO A BLACK HOLE
DEVOID OF LIGHT

After blowing the whistle on HSBC and going public in the *Reuters* news story, I was certainly not doing well financially. I was still living in a bug-infested apartment and sleeping on a camping cot. But I defined myself as successful because I was going to bring down the bad guys and make a significant and positive difference. I didn't care that by society's standards I was a complete loser. I was fighting for what was right and promoting justice. Like the "Justice is the Guardian of Liberty" engraving on the federal building in Philadelphia, I proudly slept on the camping cot because I was a *guardian*. I looked in the mirror with pride. After the *Reuters* article, I was extremely excited because I was invited to give a one-hour interview with ABC News. Brian Ross reached out to me and invited me to New York. I couldn't believe it. ABC News paid for my train tickets there because I could not afford to make the trip. I wore the same navy-blue suit that I wore to the interview at HSBC, the meeting with the FBI, and the meeting *Reuters* news team. I will never forget walking down the ABC News hallway to Brian Ross's office, which was right next to Barbara Walters's office. My heart raced as I passed by. I was hoping to meet her. Unfortunately, she was out on assignment.

Brian Ross's office had tons of golden statue awards all over the walls and his desk was huge. He was extremely nice to me. He walked me to the makeup room, where I was layered with makeup to make me not look like a vampire. At the time, I was not getting out much, and I saw very little sun. Then came the interview. It took about an hour.

Brian Ross told me it was one of the most powerful interviews he'd ever conducted and that it would air within two weeks. Two weeks went by. Nothing. I was told there were "production delays."

Meanwhile, I was also contacted by 60 Minutes, but they had to pass when they heard ABC had the story. Months came and went, and the story didn't air. My money was running out, and I was forced to ask my parents for allowance. My parents sent me $150 a week, which was just not enough. I decided to sell everything that was not an essential item. The one thing I had plenty of were my books, which I listed on eBay. The eBay profits were still not enough. I prayed that the story would air on ABC News. I knew that once ABC aired the story, HSBC would be fully exposed to the American public—and maybe some viewer would offer me a job.

There was no other way I could get a job, at that point. I was blacklisted from every bank in the United States. I did the right thing, but employers do not want to risk hiring someone who might report them to law enforcement.

My other problem came out in the ABC interview. Brian Ross asked me if I was a CIA agent and if I was planted at the bank. My answer was, of course, "No." But a lot of people thought I was a CIA agent anyway, which I was not. There is a big difference between working for the CIA and passing information to them.

The CIA never employed or paid me.

I was also not being paid by the FBI because I didn't listen to the special agent about *Reuters* using my photo. I was a federal witness but not under the official protection program. Had I been, I would have received a check. I was helping the FBI for free. The news agencies also could not pay me because of conflict of interest and journalistic integrity. Reporters can't pay sources. Overall, I had only one source of income: my mom and dad. I know my parents would have given more than $150 a week, but at the time, my dad was still battling cancer and going through intense radiation and chemotherapy. My parents had their own very serious financial problems. I was basically in a bind.

I needed the ABC story to air just to make something happen. Then came the deferred prosecution agreement (DPA), which was an agreement between the Department of Justice and HSBC. The deal was that if HSBC Bank admitted to the charge of "financing the enemy," they had to pay $1.9 billion in fines. The bank then had five years to clean up its act or the case would be reopened. Now, $1.9 billion sounds like a lot of money, but it is actually only four or five weeks of HSBC's profits. It was a slap on the wrist. Worst of all, the deferred prosecution agreement was just a monetary fine: *no jail time for anyone.* Let me make this very clear. HSBC executives admitted to the US government that they "financed the enemy" and not *one* of them went to jail. I don't know about you, but if I donated just $1 to a terrorist organization, I'm pretty sure they would send me to jail.

The real sick part was that HSBC was allowed to continue its operations. I was in a hotel room in New York the day the announcement was made. I knew a big announcement was going to be made by the Department of Justice, but I didn't know the details. I stayed in a hotel room in New York because I figured reporters and government officials would want to talk to me about the announcement. As I watched the DPA announcement on the TV in my hotel room, my heart sank. I saw Brian Ross ask a couple of questions to the speaker, but he never mentioned my name. I was devastated with the result. *How could this happen? Where is the justice? Where is the dove flying across the courtroom? Where is the Guardian of our Liberty?* I sat at the hotel room desk, staring at my cell phone. I was waiting for the ring. I sat and stared literally for about an hour. Nobody called. I picked up the phone and called the FBI special agents I was working with.

"I am sorry, Everett. We tried. Our hands are tied on this."

"Bullshit. Why don't you raid the building?"

"I know you are upset. You did the right thing, and you should be proud of yourself. We are disappointed also. We are sorry, but we can't do anything."

My heart further sank into a black hole. I was not depressed. I was angry. I was *beyond* angry. I was livid and disgusted. *This is America? Hands are tied? Unbelievable!* After another hour of waiting for the phone to never ring, I went back to my hole-in-the-wall apartment and cried myself to sleep.

I woke up the next morning faced with a cold, hard reality. If I was going to get through this, I had to believe there was still hope. The ABC News interview with Brian Ross could still air. The next day, I called Brian Ross and asked him when the story was going to air. He had been holding the tape for months.

"Everett, we decided not to run the story."

I lost my soul. Everything was gone. My anger turned to depression. The war, the fight, the quest for justice was terminated. HSBC won. All of my efforts were meaningless. It was all a waste. After being betrayed by ABC, the FBI, and the Justice Department, I could not look myself in the mirror anymore. I was not a *Guardian of Liberty*. I was a loser with nothing. My spirit was broken.

PEANUT BUTTER AND JELLY

I didn't leave my apartment for days. My diet consisted of peanut butter and jelly sandwiches and hot dogs because I couldn't afford anything else. One night, as I cut open the frozen, plastic wrapping that encased four jumbo hot dogs and plopped them into a pot of boiling water, I thought of the catered banquets the HSBC executives provided the whole staff to celebrate closing 150,000 alerts. I thought of all the different cured meats and cheeses, the caviar, and fine fruits. I thought of my colleagues still at HSBC, making $55,000 to $100,000 a year. They were probably out having dinner, celebrating not going to jail and just being fined. I imagined Burns and Traitor out this Saturday night, eating lobster, crab, and ribeye steaks while giving toasts to each other over Grey Goose vodka martinis.

My focus returned to the hot dogs boiling in the pot. This was the tenth day in a row of eating hot dogs for dinner. I began to cry. I cried because I had failed. I failed at my mission. I failed myself and the American people. I was the ultimate loser.

I remembered Burns calling me into his big "office" cubicle

several months ago and saying, "Everett, don't you see? The problems you are having with management are your fault. The problem is *you*—not them."

The hot dogs were now dancing widely in the pot as the boiling water reached its peak temperature. I said to myself, "Burns was right. *I'm* the problem." I turned the knob on the stove that controlled the burner under the hot dogs off. I left the hot dogs half-cooked in the water and walked about five steps to my fold-out, plastic desk.

I had a tiny safe on my desk, where I kept some cash and my 9mm handgun. I opened the safe, reached inside, and found the handgun. I wrapped my hand around the grip, took it out of the safe, and placed it on the desk. I sat down on my metal, fold-out chair that I used as my desk chair and picked up the gun, pressing the magazine release. The magazine fell onto the desk.

With my left hand, I pulled back the slide to see if there were any bullets in the chamber. There were none. I reinserted the loaded magazine into the gun and pulled back the slide.

The handgun was now loaded and ready to fire. I carefully set it back on the plastic desk. I sat, completely still, staring at it for a while. There was nothing left of me. I'd fought the good fight, and I'd failed. It was time to check out. At least I would be remembered for trying.

I picked up the handgun and placed it under my chin, resting my finger on the trigger and closing my eyes. Then, something amazing happened. My pet rabbit jumped up onto my lap.

Startled, I opened my eyes and put down the gun. My rabbit's name was Einstein. He was litter trained so he could hop around my apartment, free range. I looked at my pet rabbit with tears in my eyes. In that one moment, I saw the representation of pure goodness and innocence. All a rabbit does is hop around, eat vegetables, and put smiles on the faces of everyone they meet.

The moment Einstein jumped up onto my lap, I realized what I was really fighting for. It wasn't solely about HSBC. I was fighting a battle for *good*.

I was thinking too small. I realized that HSBC was just one, small cog in a giant wheel. I was now battle ready and tested. I just went up against one of the world's largest banks and made a difference—not the difference I wanted, but it was something. No matter the outcome, I still did what was right.

I'd found my purpose: *I am a fighter for the good and innocent.* Einstein sat on my lap; unaware he'd just saved my life. It was time to put HSBC behind me and move forward. I unloaded the gun and put it back in the safe.

I spent the next week journaling and researching, trying to figure out my next move. Finally, my phone did ring. On the other end was Matt Taibbi from *Rolling Stone,* wanting to do a feature on me and HSBC.

Today, I have the gun I almost killed myself with on display in my office. The gun represents my rock bottom. When you hit rock bottom, you are surrounded by darkness. There is no light. I admit that the *nothing* almost got me. I almost fell into a state of apathy and defeat. But it was in my darkest hour that I found a reason to go on.

SAVED BY P.F. CHANG'S

There is a difference between knowing your *purpose* and knowing your *why*. Everyone is born with a purpose. Some may choose to ignore it, but I believe we all have an innate purpose to make the world a better place.

The human race strives to improve itself. Yes, there will always be setbacks, but the overall purpose remains. I believe that the *why* relates to the actions of a specific individual. A person is motivated by their *why* and then takes action to achieve a specific outcome.

My *why* was formed after hitting rock bottom, in the pit of absolute darkness. Rock bottom meant losing everything, including my possessions and friends. I was utterly alone when I had the silver Kahr 9mm under my chin, before my rabbit hopped up on my lap. My purpose was still the same, even though I lost everything—I found my *why*, which was to protect innocent people from injustice.

My ascent out of the pit of darkness began moments after Einstein shocked my system and I put the gun down. The *nothing* began to lose its grip. My soul reconnected with God. And, after finding my *why*, came the critical question of, "How?"

I needed to change the system from the inside. I needed to become a congressman or a senator. I looked around at my squalid 400-square-foot apartment, and I laughed out loud at the thought. I pulled out a legal pad, took one of those old-fashioned, yellow pencils from a translucent plastic container, and armed myself with a handheld pencil sharpener. I began to journal.

Carrie took on her own mission to help me carry a food tray. She even gave me a tray to take home and practice with. She would stay late past the shift and walk around the restaurant with me holding a tray loaded with Chinese food. Management took me in. Some nights, Mark and Carrie even gave me leftover food from the kitchen to take home. They knew my situation, and all they kept saying was, "Everett, you did the right thing." The only people who helped me after blowing the whistle on HSBC were the management and waitstaff at P.F. Chang's—Mark and Carrie. Several other waiters took me under their wing as well and helped me type the customer orders into the computer. And sometimes, they'd simply provide a much-needed, friendly smile.

I learned through years of battling the *nothing*—and many of its agents—that my purpose in life is to fight against injustice. I formed my company, Tactical Rabbit, on P.F. Chang's money, so I could light the candle, illuminate the room, and have hope again.

After I became successful monetarily, I went back to P.F. Chang's and left a $1,000 tip and another $500 tip for my two favorite waiters. I love P.F. Chang's and the people I worked with because they took me in. They gave me the opportunity to fight back the *nothing* and win. But there was no crowd, no standing ovation. I had few supporters. All of my old friends had already abandoned me. And for the first time, I was okay with that.

TOO BIG TO JAIL

I n the fall of 2013, I received a call from a congressional aide to Congresswoman Maxine Waters. She was the head of the House Financing Committee. I was invited to Capitol Hill for a confidential meeting with the congresswoman. I was told to bring whatever evidence I had on HSBC. I drove down to Washington, still in my beat-up Hyundai, hoping that this meeting would be the game changer. I did not agree with Waters's politics, but that was irrelevant; she was in a position of power and could make a significant and positive difference. She was an elected official, and an outspoken one at that.

The congresswoman's office was not actually at Capitol Hill—it was a couple of buildings away, where all the senators and congressmen had their private offices. I was told by the congressional aide to bypass the giant line of reporters, aides, and general visitors waiting to go through building security by calling him.

I stood in front of the congressional office building, admiring the hefty line of people. I called the aide, and he emerged from the front doors and waved me in. I had already researched him on LinkedIn; I had his photo burned into my mind so I would recognize him immediately.

As I entered, security took notice, but the aide flashed a badge and said I was with him. Walking through the hallways, I was impressed and intimidated by the scores of reporters holding cameras and microphones. For a second, I thought I saw Brian Ross from ABC News, but then I dismissed the thought because I was sure Brian was too busy digging a grave in some park in New York and throwing my HSBC interview into the abyss.

The aide stopped and opened the giant oak doors that read, "Maxine Waters." In the main section of her office sat a receptionist.

"You must be Everett. Congresswoman Waters is in the meeting room."

Her aide led me into the room, and Congresswoman Waters stood to greet me. I could not believe it. It was an out-of-body experience. The congresswoman and I shook hands, and she directed me to sit on this giant couch.

"Make yourself comfortable," she said, as she took a seat in this antique, powerful-looking chair directly in front of me. "Everett, thank you for coming all the way to Washington. I know it is quite a trip from Philadelphia. Let me get to the point. I want to know everything about what happened at HSBC. If you have any documents or evidence, I would like to see that as well."

I explained the entire fraud and treason HSBC was committing against the US government and the American people. Waters was shocked and taken aback. She then said, "Everett, are you prepared to testify to what you are saying to the House Financing Committee?"

My heart skipped a beat. "Yes, absolutely."

"Everett, I think it's time we take HSBC down. Where are your documents?"

I pulled the documents out of my briefcase and handed them to the congressional aide. Waters stood up and went to her giant desk in the back of the room, behind her power chair. She picked up a white phone and said something I couldn't make out. As Waters sat back in her chair, a team of aides came into the room. Waters said to the team of aides, "I want you to go through all of these documents and take detailed notes. I want to brief the committee on this."

The documents were passed to one of the aides, who could not have been more than a year or two out of college. The aides rushed out of the room with lightning speed.

The congresswoman told me to wait for a call so we could arrange for a date to testify. I couldn't believe it. On my drive back home, I could not have been happier. This was it! Something was finally going to be done. I didn't care what most of my Republican friends said about Waters. She cared! And she was going to reignite the flame to take down HSBC. I waited two days and then called for a status update.

The aide answered the phone abruptly and was not as friendly as before I made the trip. "We are still going through the documents." I waited another week and still didn't hear anything, so I called again. No answer, so I left a voicemail. After two or three days, there was no return call. I decided to leave a message with Waters's secretary directly to see if there was a tentative date they thought I would testify.

The receptionist took down the message, but there was no reply. Waters went silent for two months. Then I read online that Congresswoman Maxine Waters had just introduced a new anti-money laundering bill to the House floor. The bill had nothing to do with HSBC. The bill was meant to stiffen the penalties for individuals who launder money. The bill was based on my HSBC evidence and conversation with her. Waters received tremendous attention for this bill, and it helped her political agenda. I realized that the congresswoman had no intention of facing off against HSBC. My evidence, documents, and verbal description of the treason I witnessed were just to put a new bill on the House floor. There was not going to be any testifying before the committee.

I had been used. I had been used for information to advance her agenda and score political points. Maxine Waters's office never did get back to me. They had what they wanted and there was no need for me anymore. After reading about the bill on my computer monitor, I bowed my head. I'd been played.

I was devastated, because for a short time, I really thought Congresswoman Waters was going to fight against HSBC. I thought incorrectly that I established a powerful alliance. I was wrong. Maxine Waters did me a big favor, though—she made me realize that I must become an elected public official. It was the congressmen and senators who held the true power to make a significant, positive difference. If I wanted to make a real change for the good of society and really serve as a *Guardian of Liberty*, I had to become a congressman or senator myself and change the system from the inside.

On August 29, 2013, before meeting with Waters, I held a major HSBC protest at the steps of the New York Public Library, a couple of blocks away from HSBC's HQ in New York City. I gave an impassioned speech with members of Occupy Wall Street at my back, holding anti-HSBC signs. I went to the leaders of Occupy Wall Street for help because I needed a support base.

At first, the members of Occupy Wall Street were extremely resistant to helping a young Republican, but I said in an Occupy meeting at Columbia University, "I disagree with 99 percent of the things you believe in, but the enemy of my enemy is my friend. We share a common enemy. Join me, and we will fight against HSBC Bank together."

Occupy Wall Street saw my sincerity in putting our differences aside and decided to support me at the August 29th protest. Occupy Wall Street held up their end of the bargain by coming out in full force, and in return, I went to the Occupy Wall Street anniversary protest a few months later. I am a full supporter of Occupy Wall Street—not their political views, but their willingness to fight for their beliefs. They were out there with signs protesting and trying to raise awareness about the injustice on Wall Street. They supported me at my protest when nobody else would. I am not a political supporter of Occupy Wall Street, but I respect them and will never forget how they helped me. I knew then that I needed to run for office. Even though I respect Occupy Wall Street, they have their strategy all wrong. The change can only come from inside the system. I have little respect for Waters. She was in a position of power and wasn't using it correctly. But her strategy was correct. She had real power to instill change. It appeared to me that she was out for political points and not necessarily the greater good.

For days after I realized I'd been played, I was in deep contemplation about the United States political system. All I read about was politicians trying to score political points. There is tremendous corruption and a high level of self-advancement. During the HSBC scandal, there were Senate hearings where HSBC executives testified and admitted to sponsoring terrorism. The senators put on a grand show of reaming out the HSBC executives, but did the committee actually do anything? No action was taken. All the senators cared about was looking good to their constituents. Where was the justice? All of these senators and congressmen were out for themselves. They did not care about the greater good. They cared about getting reelected. The idea to run for office began to solidify in my brain. A feeling of fear came over me. I started asking myself extremely negative questions: What if I run, and nobody take me seriously? What if I run for office and lose? What if I just end up making a total ass out of myself?

I then asked the most important question of all: What if I *don't* run for office?

I closed my eyes and teleported back in time, again staring at the HSBC Wire Filter with all dots and dashes in the terrorist's and their accomplices' names so the wires would go through. I saw the hundreds upon millions of dollars in wires to terrorist organizations and drug cartels on my HSBC computer screen. I saw the hundreds of debt collectors clicking their mouses, closing alert after alert, and subsequently allowing terrorists to receive their funds. Then I saw a TV with a CNN reporter saying, "Another plane just crashed into the Twin Towers!" as a fireball consumed one of the towers, killing thousands. I saw an Iraq war vet with no legs outside the VA hospital where my dad worked, his legs lost in a roadside bomb. I said to myself, "Everett, you have to risk looking like an ass. You have to risk not being taken seriously. You have to risk *losing.*"

I was still not committed to running for office until I read online that HSBC was donating to the campaign of Senator Pat Toomey. HSBC Bank actually formed a PAC and was buying congressmen and senators with donations to their campaigns. My rage did not set in until I read that Senator Pat Toomey sat on the Senate Banking Committee.

That's right: HSBC was donating to the campaign of a senator who determined their fate. He was one of the senators who helped let HSBC off the hook! When I lost everything and was waiting tables for $2.15 an hour, this senator was eating fancy dinners and letting a bank that was sponsoring terrorism off the hook. Now, there was no choice but to run for office. This was no longer about politics. This was personal. I had to run for United States Senate. The odds were against me a million to one, but it didn't matter if I lost and made an ass out of myself. I had to make a statement. I had to show the American public that David would still stand against Goliath.

OUT OF THE ASHES

Back when I was an idealistic intern working on Wall Street, an executive said to me one day, "Everett, nobody cares. Nobody cares about your life; nobody cares about you." This was followed by a litany of *nobody cares*, intoned like some medieval chant and ending with, "It all comes down to the dollar." Cynical, yes—but with a kernel of truth. To be an agent of change for the good, I needed to be financially solvent. I needed to start a business and make it successful. But what type of business? What service would someone pay for? Starting a business—as I was to discover—is a process of trial and error. It is also a process of objective, rational introspection and, above all, persistence and belief.

My first venture was to create a website. The site had articles written by writers paid out of my earnings as a waiter. The business plan, as such, was that as people subscribed and the site gained traction, it would eventually attract sponsors.

That didn't work; nobody subscribed.

Switching gears, I trained my sights on investigative-type job postings listed on the Internet. At the time, my overhead was very low—no office, just a plastic desk in my apartment and a computer with an Internet connection. I started to get projects.

Effectively, I became a freelance intelligence broker. To get the work done, I reached out to former CIA and FBI people on LinkedIn, introduced myself, and contracted with them. Encouraged by the early successes, I took an office, hired an analyst, began a marketing campaign, and started sending out letters and mailers. No responses. I let the analyst go. Soon, I had to let the office go. I was broke—back in my apartment and back to working at P.F. Chang's. I needed to do something different.

I thought long and hard about why no one responded to the emails, letters, and mailers that I'd sent out and came to the conclusion that people just saw it as junk mail and threw it away. What I needed was a more personal touch—no marketing. Instead, I sent out certified mail letters to prospective clients. Who wouldn't open a certified letter addressed to them? I began getting responses, a few projects here and there. Friends suggested that I should approach law firms and get a retainer. I sent out countless certified mail letters to law firms, but none wanted to pay. It was time to switch strategies again. What other resource had I not tapped? Though I got no financial benefit from the HSBC scandal, I did acquire another kind of currency—name recognition. I began scouring newspapers for stories about people needing help. I sent out certified letters, offering to be an advocate and expose fraud and corruption. Be a David standing beside them, fighting the Goliath. It worked. People saw me as a media guy, a whistleblower, someone willing to go down the rabbit hole—a Tactical Rabbit.

TRADECRAFT

Tactical Rabbit is a private intelligence agency. The most common misconception about what we do is that people think we are a private investigation firm. Nothing could be further from the truth. Tactical Rabbit is like a private CIA. In a sense, we have more freedom than government agencies as we answer only to our clients. Those clients could be a law firm representing a plaintiff in a case of technology theft, they could be a company seeking asset recovery where a debtor hid funds and claims to be bankrupt, or a company seeking to buy another company and wanting to know if there are any skeletons in the closet that might come back and bite them. The nature of the work we do sometimes involves crossing paths with dangerous criminal elements, such as drug dealers, terrorists, and other outlaws on the dark web.

Diving deep down the rabbit hole of private intelligence work requires using CIA-type tradecraft. The people who work at Tactical Rabbit—retired CIA, FBI, and other intelligence professionals—are experts at it.

There are a few basic rules to intelligence tradecraft, some of which seem counterintuitive.

The first is: *be your true self.* The common notion of undercover work is that you have to blend in. If you create a fictional character, you have to create a web of lies, and you have to remember all those lies. That is setting yourself up to fail. Another misconception is that you turn off your cellphone when overseas to hide your location. That sends up a red flag—a cellphone can be tracked, even if turned off.

Airports and ports of entry are heavily monitored by foreign intelligence agencies and criminal gangs. Russian, Chinese, and organized crime cyber capabilities are far ahead of those in the US. Never plug in a computer or phone to a USB connection in an airport. It takes just a minute for a bad actor to slip in a chip or replace the connection, and seconds after you plug in, your information is copied. When you travel with a computer or USB drive overseas, make sure it has nothing but the operating system on it. The contents of the computer can be scanned even if the device is not plugged in or turned on.

Hotels overseas can be a minefield for US citizens. One of the most sought-after items to steal is a US passport. Leaving your travel documents in your room is an invitation to have them lifted. In countries such as the Dominican Republic and Mexico, some of the resorts are owned by drug and other criminal cartels. But this isn't a problem for just hotels and resorts—nightclubs and entertainment venues can hold hidden risks, too. One time, at a club in London, while having a social drink with business colleagues, a hostess tried lifting my passport from my back pocket. The ensuing melee ended up with the bouncers throwing us out, covered in cuts and bruises, but my passport was still in my possession. That is how precious it is; you have to fight to hold onto it.

Many of these intelligence operations require operating under a commercial cover. That entails setting up a shell company with an office—someone to answer the phones, a professional website, creating email addresses, business cards, a social media presence, and more. Unlike government intelligence agencies that also use commercial cover for operations, private intelligence operatives are on their own. You can never be sure if the next meeting will be your last.

In the course of our work, we often uncover information that presents an ethical quandary. Do we ignore it, as it is not what we are being paid for? Or do we follow up on our own dollar and pass the information onto law enforcement or other government agencies? A portion of the profits from assignments undertaken by Tactical Rabbit is used to fund independent intelligence work that is not paid for by clients but undertaken purely in the interests of national security.

MISSION

Tactical Rabbit acquires clients in a myriad of ways. We search news articles for stories that could use our services. Sometimes we get a tip, other times it is the result of a lawsuit. Or a business wishes to check out the background of a potential partner investment. Sometimes, a family member reaches out for us handle a delicate family relationship. Wealthy families are often targeted by criminals. Such was the case that brought me to Rome via Tel Aviv and Germany.

The scion of a wealthy family had married a stunning model from Ukraine. They asked us to investigate her background. What we found was that she was already married to a Ukrainian mobster with connections to Russian intelligence. Bank records showed that large sums were moving from their joint bank account to her homeland. We shared our findings with the appropriate government law enforcement and intelligence agencies; they too were concerned, but felt it wasn't something that involved a national security threat. I felt they were missing an opportunity. The young man in question had extensive computer software talents and operated a blockchain for cyber currency. This gave him valuable insights into where criminal and terrorist funds were being moved.

The combination of wealth, a honey trap, and information that could be used to track down illegal money laundering and the funding of terrorists made him a sitting target to meet an untimely end. I felt, with this type of leverage, it may be possible to convince this young man that he could be a valuable intelligence asset to the United States.

We arranged to meet in a small-town location. I was nervous. Doing this self-directed meant setting up an entire intel security arrangement, that if anything went wrong, government agencies could claim plausible deniability. We didn't know if he was being tailed, but we had to hope for the best and plan for the worst. He was standing on the side of the road when we picked him up. We began driving fast through the narrow winding streets and alleyways, making sure there was no one following us, stopping eventually at a restaurant. Inside, I had arranged for "guests" to surreptitiously take photos of everyone coming in and out of the place so we would have a visual record of those present.

The two of us got a table and had lunch, filled with small talk. He smoked incessantly. After the meal, I suggested we go for a walk in a local park that we had checked out earlier. It was the perfect place to speak—a circular-shaped walking path with water splashing loudly in the middle. There, I told him what we had found out about his "wife" and the danger that he was facing. He was stunned. I told him that if he wanted, we could get him out of the country to safety.

He asked for forty-eight hours to think it over. After we parted, I rode to the airport and bought a ticket for the first available flight to Spain to rest up and appear to be a tourist taking in the sites for a few days. Later, we heard that he and his wife parted. What happened after that, I have no idea. As far as the client was concerned, it was mission accomplished.

SWEET BRIAR COLLEGE AND THE QUEST FOR JUSTICE

The *nothing* is an all-powerful force that will always be in existence. The *nothing* represents apathy and a world devoid of the light we all need in our lives to nourish our souls. The *nothing*, which I have consistently battled in my own life, does not act alone. The *nothing* has agents.

There are very real people who want you to be apathetic, who want to suck you into a culture of pure disregard. They have a very clear agenda to turn you into a person of apathy because, if you are devoid of light and have no hope, then you are easier to control. And the people who have control have all the power.

Before May of 2015, I had never even heard of Sweet Briar College.

I was having lunch with a few money managers and investment bankers at the high roller spot Capital Grille when the topic of Sweet Briar College was first brought to my attention. As I sat there, being waited on by super-trained waiters who were constantly filling up our glasses with Pellegrino, I had a flashback of waiting tables and being covered in Chinese food.

But my flashback was suddenly interrupted by one of the investment bankers asking me, "Everett, can you do some digging on this guy? There is a situation, and I am curious what you can find."

"What kind of situation?"

"It involves the college my wife went to."

"Of course. When do you need the intel by?"

"Whenever you get to it. This is just out of curiosity. This isn't official or anything."

The not being "official" meant I was not going to get paid. The money did not matter, though, as it was important to score points with this guy. Wall Street was a tightknit community, and maybe I could get a referral later on. He wrote a name on the back of his card and handed it to me. I looked at the name and had no idea who it was. I also did not know that the investment banker's curious request would insert me into an all-out war.

I researched the name and the situation on my laptop, on the Amtrak coming back from Wall Street. After reading about the situation and this person—who was the president of Sweet Briar College—I immediately knew I had to find a way to help. The Sweet Briar students were the absolute representation of pure goodness and innocence. The research and time that I would have to put into this was going to cost me serious money. The next day, I sent an email to the banker letting him know that I needed to be paid to conduct an in-depth investigation.

I received an email in a five-minute turnaround time politely telling me to go take a hike. Now I had a problem. If I took on this case, I was going to have to invest my own money into it with no return. From a business standpoint, this was a no-go. A business exists to make a profit not to lose money. The theoretical existence of my company was to make a profit, but the actual existence and founding principle was to protect pure goodness and innocence. As I paced around my office, I remembered my

MBA professors preaching, "The CEO's job is the maximization of shareholder wealth."

I had investors, so ethically—according to my professors—I needed to maximize their shareholder wealth. But I did not form my company purely for profit. I lost everything once before, and I could do it again. I attribute my success to fighting with nothing to lose.

Forget shareholder wealth. The reason I was getting clients and growing my company was because I was not after the buck—I was after sincerity and helping people. I had to help the Sweet Briar students. But what if they didn't want my help? It was a risk I had to take. First, I needed to invest in an in-depth investigation, and even see if I could find a secret weapon for the students to use.

I had to figure out the motivation. Why shut down a school with no notice when there was plenty of money? If more money was needed, why was the administration not accepting donations from loyal alumni trying to keep the school open? Money was not the issue. There had to be an agenda. But who would want to wipe Sweet Briar College off of the map and kill the hopes and dreams of its students? In May of 2015, the *nothing* was winning. It looked like the Sweet Briar women were about to see the scales of "justice" tip out of their favor.

I called up other members of my team and we went to work. It took about a week, but then we came to our derived conclusion. We believed with a high degree of confidence that it was a land grab. It was very odd that the senior admins were heavily connected to very large defense contracting firms looking for new facilities.

Even if I was wrong in the exact reason for the administration suddenly wanting to shut the school down, I sensed that something was off. It just did not make logical sense to close the school with very little notice and while still having plenty of funds. Sweet Briar was not going bankrupt.

In the early stages of the Sweet Briar war, the Attorney General of Virginia was on the side of the administration. It wasn't until much later, when the students and alumni roared to a point that could not be ignored, that he supported the school. It was very odd to me that the Attorney General was so adamant in defending the administration and allowing the school to close. The farther I went down the rabbit hole, the more I realized that I had to do something. But *what* could I do? The only thing I could do was help bring the spotlight on the administration and get the general public to realize this was not just a Virginia problem but an American problem as well.

The closing of Sweet Briar College would be a major injustice to its students—therefore, it eroded liberty and American values. The Sweet Briar war represented the fight for what is right. I reached out to several of its students and told them I wanted to help. The students were welcoming and supportive. I gave a press conference in May of 2015, desperately trying to put heat on the administration and draw in public support for the students. This was the first time I took a public stand for a situation other than HSBC.

The following is my letter to the FBI that I wrote in absolute desperation for the Sweet Briar women:

May 10, 2015
VIA US MAIL / PUBLIC POST
James Comey, Director
Federal Bureau of Investigation 935 Pennsylvania Avenue, NW Washington, D.C. 20535-0001
Re: Federal Investigation: Sweet Briar College Closing

Director Comey,
    This letter is out of extreme concern regarding the events surrounding the closure of Sweet Briar College. A confidential intelligence submission alerted my intelligence officers of possible

fraud and criminal malfeasance within the Sweet Briar College administration. In response, Tactical Rabbit launched HUMINT Intelligence Operations in defense of the Sweet Briar Community. The intelligence due diligence process yielded disturbing results indicating Sweet Briar Board Chair Paul G. Rice recruited President James Jones with the intention of dissolving the college without advanced good faith notification to the Sweet Briar Community. With a high degree of confidence, we believe that Rice and Jones violated Federal Law via fraudulent concealment by accepting and recruiting students while actively being engaged in a plan to dissolve the college. The Sweet Briar criminal diamond is complex with many facets; however, the newly built gym and library elucidate just a small example of the intention to deceive.

Moreover, I hold the creed that there is substantial evidence of fraudulent concealment via the federal student loans and the subsequent financial crime committed against the students. No attempt is being made to refund the students who were duped into attending a college that presented the intentions of staying open for years to come.

Further illuminating the facets of the criminal diamond, a confidential source revealed accounting documents are being manipulated and shredded. With a medium to high degree of confidence, Tactical Rabbit believes that Chairman of the Board Paul G. Rice is manipulating the true financial condition of the college and then providing the lower board members with false intelligence in which to make decisions on. The driving motivation of the illegal actions appear to be due to a land deal. Tactical Rabbit believes with a high degree of confidence that the land will be converted into a quasi-federal facility similar to the Verizon Government partnership about 90 miles north. It was ascertained in intelligence operation that the Chairman of the Board, Paul G. Rice, has indirect exposure to his former companies and associates who are being awarded federal government contracts via the Homeland Security Eagle II program. With a high degree of confidence, Rice is using the Rice Family Foundation, which is owned by his wife, to make investments into his former associates firms. Our hypothesis is supported by the fact that Rice has shrunk most of the Sweet Briar staff but has brought on a key IT and wireless expert from Stetson University. It appears that the college is "going under," yet beefing up its IT capabilities. Recently, Rice's previous companies have received numerous federal contracts for wireless intel and mission critical operations. I am also extremely concerned about the president of the college, James Jones, who previously drained a college endowment and has numerous nefarious allegations against him. Adding to the accusations, Tactical Rabbit believes with a high degree of confidence that Rice and Jones possibly participated in bond manipulation, which would also fall under federal jurisdiction.

Exacerbating an already egregious situation, the Virginia Attorney General appears to have interests within the same sphere as Rice; therefore, there may be a possible conflict of interest. The aforementioned conjecture may be the reason why the VA Attorney General has not launched formal investigations despite the outrageous facts of the situation and public outcry for accountability and transparency. Due to the mission critical defense contracting of Rice's interest, a special investigation unit may be needed to investigate this matter. I do not believe the VA Attorney General can provide the Sweet Briar community a fair and impartial approach to justice.

During the Save Sweet Briar Press Conference on 05/09/15, a young woman student issued a plea for help from the crowd (seen in the press conference video) because she was being threatened by the Sweet Briar administration and staff. She was afraid to fight for her college, classmates, and justice in fear of retaliation. This courageous student told the world that Sweet Briar staff have been intimating and threatening students. I am personally saddened and outraged that the young women of Sweet Briar College are not receiving the support that they need and deserve.

Furthermore, Sweet Briar College can be saved and remain open as long as the Sweet Briar administration is stopped from intentionally driving the school bus off a cliff. I have personally seen the strength of these young women and they can rise like a phoenix from the ashes. I am respectfully asking for the Federal Bureau of Investigation to give these young women a chance by launching an investigation. Justice must prevail. We must ensure the good guys win in the end. Outside of the federal courthouse, engraved on the wall, it says, "Justice is the Defense of our Freedoms." The illegal shutdown of Sweet Briar College is placing all of our freedoms in jeopardy. If Sweet Briar College dies, then a piece of America will die with her.

Sincerely,
Everett A. Stern, MBA
CEO & Intelligence Director
Tactical Rabbit Inc.
United States of America

I took the Sweet Briar case very personally. It was hard when some of the students who actually supported the administration were posting negative comments online about me. I remember being upset after a blogger posted a negative article. I was hurt because I had so much invested—not just money, but my heart. I really cared, because the closing of the school was just wrong. There was no gray area on this one. This was black and white. The line crossing into the wrong was well overstepped. In the end, the Attorney General had a sudden change of heart, the administrators resigned, and the school stayed open.

The Sweet Briar scandal was one of the hardest cases my company took on. I spent tens of thousands of dollars of my own money to pay for an investigation into the administration. Countless hours were spent analyzing intelligence and uncovering the fraud that the administration was committing against the students. Overall, my press conference and intelligence report did not save Sweet Briar, but it put the administration on the defensive and applied tremendous public pressure to keep the school open.

Did I save Sweet Briar college? Absolutely not. The Sweet Briar students and alumni, with extreme tenacity, saved the school. They were relentless and defended themselves with honor. All I did was put a little more spotlight on the administration and hopefully showed the students that people outside of their college community cared about our overall liberties being eroded if the school was closed. That was the purpose of opening Tactical Rabbit—to be on the right side of the fight. I pray we made some kind of a difference, but it doesn't matter. What matters is that justice prevailed, and the young women of Sweet Briar College can continue to wear their school colors with honor and pride.

ACCEPTING THE CHALLENGE

After announcing my candidacy, challenging incumbent Republican Senator Pat Toomey for United States Senate, I bought a ticket to a dinner sponsored by the Republican Party. I was not invited. My fellow Republicans hated me because I was challenging the incumbent. I wasn't taken seriously and certainly looked like an ass, but I had to fight.

The cocktail room was full of all these stuffy, rich, uptight, and fraternity-like people. Overall, it was not a friendly crowd, and I was certainly not welcome. Holding a martini in my hand, trying to blend in, I bumped into a congressman whose name I will not mention. I asked him, "What advice would you give to a young person running for office?"

"Just make the public think that you care."

Just as the congressman made the above statement, another member of the party walked up to him, shook his hand, and started talking about raising money for his campaign. I took a few steps over to the server, placed my full martini on the tray, and walked out of the cocktail room. I headed for the parking lot. I had to get out of there. I felt like I was going to throw up. I got in my car and slammed my fist on my steering wheel. *I do care! Make them think that I care? What? Screw these people! This is why I am running. I actually care!*

I drove home determined as ever to win the race against the traitor Senator Pat Toomey. He was just one of the many politicians making the public think he cared. If he really cared, then why accept money from a bank that actually and literally admitted to financing the enemy (i.e., sponsoring terrorism)? I learned from being shunned and cast out at the Republican dinner that I was not going to be supported.

To hell with them; I had to fight this one out. I was not able to raise any money because all of the Republicans were supporting my opponent. Considering the Senate race was very personal to me, I decided to self-finance my campaign. If those stuffy elitists in that cocktail room were not going to support me, then I would use my own money and do it myself.

I spent over $50,000 fighting Senator Toomey in the primary. I campaigned hard, and I lost hard as well. I was destroyed in the primary. I didn't care. I was now David, and there was still a chance I could throw a stone and hit Senator Toomey between the eyes. After I lost the primary, I continued the fight by running as an independent candidate.

The chances of me winning the US Senate race in Pennsylvania in 2016 were astronomically low. I was up against an entrenched senator with millions of dollars in the bank. So why run? The answer is because politics shouldn't be about winning or losing. It should be about getting the message out, and my message was, "WE ARE NOT GOING TO BE SOLD OUT ANYMORE!"

It was a major symbol of hope that the HSBC whistleblower—who lost everything in defense of the United States—stood up to a senator financed by the HSBC Bank PAC.

Did I waste $50,000 to $75,000 of my own money? No, I didn't.

It can be said that David stood up to Goliath. In this dark world of apathy and indifference, a light must shine to prove that caring still exists, no matter how dim that light is.

When I ran, I promised all of my supporters that I would go down fighting, with honor, and that is exactly what I did. I refused to cave the way Bernie Sanders did. I refused to endorse someone I hated just because I was told to. I did not sell out.

THE ACCIDENT

I had run against Senator Pat Toomey in 2016 and lost. I had not expected to win; beating a sitting member of the US Senate is an uphill battle. My reasons for entering the fray were to register my displeasure at his accepting funds from an HSBC political action committee and the fact that no one at the bank had been sentenced to any jail time for what amounted to a treasonous act of laundering billions in terrorist funds.

After the election, I decided to take a vacation. In January 2017, I flew down to West Palm Beach, Florida. One day during my stay, I was talking on my phone while sitting in the back of a chauffeured town car when suddenly I heard a crash and was flung forward from my seat. It was a relatively low-impact collision, but it didn't feel like it.

My back and leg took the worst of the impact. Shaken, aching, but grateful that the accident was not life-threatening, I made my way back to my hotel and decided to stay a couple of extra days to rest up.

The pain in my leg and back did not improve. They were getting worse. When I returned to

Pennsylvania, I set up an appointment to see a neurosurgeon. He did a series of MRIs and told me that I had a major disc herniation and the pain in my legs was due to sciatica. He told me a simple fusion operation would solve the pain; I would be out of it for three or four days.

I called my parents to ask them to come up—no one likes to face an operation alone—but they could not make it. So, I decided to go ahead with the operation alone. When I woke up, I was in excruciating pain. I couldn't move. My left leg was paralyzed. During the operation, when they put a plate in my lower back, one of the screws had hit a nerve.

For me to be able to walk again, I would need rehab—literally to learn to walk again using my left leg.

The insurance company thought otherwise. The hospital refused to release me without rehab and the insurance company refused to green-light it. The reason they gave was that during physical therapy, I had managed to walk three painful steps too many. If I hadn't gritted my teeth and told myself to forget the pain for those three steps, they would have paid for rehab.

The hospital eventually relented and finally sent me home with a prescription for fifteen milligrams of OxyContin to be taken every four hours. I was alone, with no help and a bottle of pills. Unable to move around, I stopped eating. A blood clot formed in my left leg—then another. The mixture of opioids and no food put me into a state of confusion. I didn't know who I was or where I was. A nurse who was sent to check on me rushed me to the hospital. They force-fed me sugar to bring me around.

I couldn't handle trying to recuperate alone; I needed help. I wrote a post asking for help and put it up on my Facebook page. One person responded: Valerie Hall, my old high school teacher, the same woman who helped me handle the death of my closest friend all those years ago.

She flew up from Florida and stayed with me for a month; she cooked all of my food and took care of me. There are only a few good people like Valerie in this world—they inspire and uplift us and restore our faith in humanity by being just who they are.

Six months later, I had a second operation to take the metal plate out. This time, I lined up nurses and other help. The operation reduced the pain, but my back was still not right. I had gnawing, low-level pain all day. At the time, without realizing it, I was getting addicted to pain killers.

I remember taking a plane to visit a client. At the airport, I was picked up by a driver I had known for years. He looked at me, saw the pinpoint pupils in my eyes caused by the OxyContin, and told me I was messed up and that if I didn't get some help and stop taking the pain killers, things would get really bad. I signed up for an AA meeting.

In the meeting, I heard stories similar to mine and what had subsequently happened to them. My doctor was prescribing me ninety pills at a time and wanted to put me on an even more powerful opioid. This is why we have an opioid crisis. Doctors just keep writing out more and more prescriptions. Sitting in that room, I saw the price that was paid for riding that train. People who had lost everything—family, friends, possessions, and their dignity. Some of them had ended up in jail. I was there for two hours, listening to their stories. They were telling me I was an addict, just like them. I got up, left the meeting, and told myself, "This is not going to be me." When I got home, I flushed every pill down the toilet. Then came the withdrawal symptoms. They were horrible—anxiety attacks, stomach cramps, agitation, and sweating, to name a just a few.

To overcome this, I travelled down to Arizona, took a house out in the middle of nowhere, and went mountain biking. Anything to get my mind off the constant psychological and physical symptoms of withdrawals. My doctor prescribed clonidine—an antihypertensive that reduces the blood pressure and anxiety associated with withdrawal symptoms—and Ativan, an antianxiety medicine that gave me horrible nightmares. Gradually, I overcame it. I still have back pain, but I just live with it with the help of concierge medicine and a regime of physical exercise.

Through all this, my company Tactical Rabbit was shut down. I had been through hell and lost a lot of money, all brought on by the car accident. My lawyers called the limo company to account. As part of the discovery process, we obtained surveillance footage from a dashcam the company had running in the car. Apparently, every vehicle had been equipped with one to keep track of their drivers. The video of my accident made me furious. It was clear from the footage that for thirty seconds before the crash, the driver was typing on his iPad and paying no attention to the road. It was simple criminal negligence. The back and forth between my lawyers and theirs dragged on. The lawyers for the company decided to play hardball, threatening to release negative stories and make my life hell—again. I didn't care and was used to being threatened by far bigger companies. In late May 2021, we filed a case for punitive damages.

I didn't ask for any particular sum of money; I asked to send a message: If you text and drive and it hurts or kills someone, there is a price to pay—a price the jury will decide on. I still believe that justice wins out in the end.

IN THE BELLY OF THE BEAST

The Smithfield Fire Hall is an unremarkable, low-slung, white building off Route 22 in Huntingdon, Pennsylvania. My three-hour drive to this out-of-the way place from West Chester was filled with a mixture of excitement and apprehension. On this Friday evening, in late April, the Huntingdon County Republican Committee was holding its spring dinner, with three hundred at-tendees, including twenty-one committee chairmen—none of who wanted or even knew that Everett Stern was planning to attend. That is, except for Arnie McClure, who was reputed to be a nasty piece work and a hardline Trump supporter, but who had agreed to let me come as long as I paid $1,500 as a sponsor.

That in itself was an accomplishment. For the past three months, my every attempt to get traction for my US Senate campaign was blocked or stymied.

Every American citizen has the right to run for political office. This sounds good in theory and should be straightforward. The whole American political system is supposed to be about equality and giving people a fair shake. You announce your candidacy, make speeches, raise money, campaign, and let the voters decide. In practice, nothing could be further from the truth. The candidates are selected by an elite few of the ultrawealthy. Those who attempt to enter the fray uninvited face fierce resistance. Which brings me to the question: Why was I putting myself through such an ordeal?

In October 2020, Senator Pat Toomey, the US Senator for Pennsylvania, announced he would not run for reelection. This sent shockwaves through the political establishment, as Pennsylvania is a "purple" state—meaning the party that wins the soon-to-be vacant seat in Pennsylvania would take control of the Senate. I had my own reasons for running; I felt that the outgoing Senator Toomey was corrupt. In 2016, I made my first attempt to challenge for his seat. It was more of a symbolic protest effort. I knew that sitting senators were very hard to unseat, but with him gone, I had a real shot at winning—so why not exercise my constitutional right and throw my hat in the ring?

I spoke with some people about it, and they told me it was a long shot. "Your every dirty secret is going to be outed. This could destroy your life and your business." They made it very clear to me that the cons greatly outweighed the pros, but I thought, *Let's throw caution to the wind!* Through a friend, I was set up with a Federal Election Commission compliance firm.

The FEC enforces federal campaign finance laws, including monitoring donations. I thought I had hired lawyers, but over time, I discovered they were just bookkeepers. They did find for me a campaign manager—the head of faith-based initiative for the Republican Party. Later, I found out they all knew each other and were friends. Getting set up to run a political campaign costs money, in my case around $100,000. For which, I got nothing. The problems started with their messaging plan. Their goal was to position me as a Trump supporter, which I am not. I am a Commonsense, Conservative Republican, and I share very little in common with Trump Republicans. This put me in an ethical bind.

I sought out a high-powered general I knew and asked for his advice. He told me, "Everett, don't sell your soul and your reputation for a seat. Don't do it." My run for the Senate seemed over before it had begun. I had no traction, a campaign team that was not interested in promoting me, and by the end of March, I was faced with making the first quarter filing to the FEC. Failure to do so would result in a fine or jail time. I had lost all faith with the compliance firm. With the clock ticking down to less than seventy-two hours before the filing deadline, I reached out to the woman who helped me with my FEC numbers six years earlier. Though she was swamped with work, she put together a team and got my filing in before the deadline. They saved me. It felt like a gift from God. When you hit a low point and then others step in, it has the effect of lifting you up; it gives you renewed hope and encouragement. I decided to start all over again and rebuild my campaign team from scratch.

After talking with a longtime friend and lawyer, we agreed to find a new FEC compliant firm in Washington, DC. We settled on a well-respected and pricey law firm; they even found me a new campaign manager. He was only twenty-four years old. At first, I was reluctant. How could someone so young know how to run a Senate campaign? The law firm pointed out to me that I was faced with running a nontraditional campaign. There was a need to build a grassroots campaign. They told me, "Everett, trust us, this is what you need. You need a young guy who understands the grassroots effort, that will energize young people. You need to do a Barack Obama–type campaign. These young people are different; they come from wealthy families, they want to be politically active, they work hard, learn the ropes, and at some point in time, run for office themselves." They were right. A forty-something Republican operative would run a traditional campaign, like my opponents. I needed to take a different approach.

One thing I was not expecting was the amount of work that campaigning entails. I thought it would be making speeches and doing media interviews. My campaign handlers were saying, "No, no. You are going to spend three hours a day on the phone, asking people for money." I have always paid my own way, stood on my own two feet; asking people for money made me feel like a homeless person. However, surprisingly soon, it felt like just another day on the campaign trail.

One early lesson that came as a surprise and a disappointment was that people who were complete strangers, who didn't know me from Adam, were more likely to give me money and support my campaign than the people I knew well. That was very weird.

In fact, it made me angry and depressed. Over the years, I have learned to turn those disappointments and that anger into positive energy. And I needed to be positive; I needed to figure out how to get on the list of Republican committee chairmen.

The person who guarded and dispensed this list was Lawrence Tabas, Chairman of the Republican Party of Pennsylvania. As I quickly found out, he had no intention of releasing the list to me.

Shortly after I filed with the FEC, I called him. No reply. After repeated calls, I finally got him on the phone. He told me I had to be vetted, that a background check was needed. He asked me how much money I was going to put in the race. So, I said, "Look, there will be a significant amount." He said, "Check back in a couple of weeks and see if you passed the test," then added a warning for me not to contact the county chairmen on my own. I asked my campaign manager at the time if this was appropriate, if this was a normal conversation. He told me, "No, Everett, this is not good." I asked, "Why is this not good?" and he said, "I guess this means they're against you. From the start, Tabas should have given you the list. The list is given to every candidate who enters the race so they have a fair shake."

Two weeks passed, and I heard nothing. I tried calling him but got no reply. Time was passing, and I was getting nowhere.

The only option I had was to find the contact information on these chairmen and call them myself—warning or no warning.

My company, Tactical Rabbit, was a business intelligence agency, so I put some of my employees to work on getting the numbers of the chairmen and began cold-calling. None replied. I was blocked from getting into any events. Then, one chairman did reply—Arnie McClure. I asked him to give me a chance. He did.

So, on a late April evening, with the events of the past three months rollercoasting around in my brain, I parked my car and made for the entrance. I didn't know what to expect. I thought maybe it would be a crowd of local Republicans listening to a few speakers. It turned out to be a meeting of top Republicans that lasted three days, with the media barred from coming. Lawrence Tabas was there, as was the head of the Republican National Committee. When the chance arose, I grabbed the microphone. There are times in life when you get one shot to make something happen. Often, nothing comes of it. You give it your best try, and it falls short. But once in a while, you hit a home run.

On that night, I hit a home run.

Rather than praise, bow, and scrape to the political glitterati, I went on the attack. I told them, "The biggest insider threat to this country is corruption. I stand for transparency, justice, and accountability." I accused them of selling out the people of the United States. "The Republican Party is not operated for the people by the people. Everyone is being endorsed, everyone is being backed, everyone is being bought." At one point, someone tried to grab the microphone away from me. This led to calls to let me speak, and before long, there were cheers. By the end of my seven-minute speech, I received applause and a standing ovation.

I walked over to the table Lawrence Tabas was sitting at and said, "You hear that crowd. Now give me the list." For the next three days, I asked. When I spoke with the other chairpersons and other attendees, I told them Tabas would not give me the list. Some questioned why he wasn't giving me the list, while others said it was plain wrong. I deserved a fair shot. One of those who felt I deserved a fair shot was Arnie McClure.

One evening, as other speeches were underway, I found Arnie sitting by himself at a table outside of the main room. I went and sat next to him. Arnie is an old man, probably in his late seventies. He started telling me stories about his experiences in Vietnam. How a rocket went off by his head and he couldn't hear. He was a half-deaf. People assumed he yelled because he was old and grouchy, but the truth was that he'd lost his hearing serving his country. I realized the guy was actually a very kind man. "Everett," he said, "I wanted you to come out here. I wanted to give you a fair shake." He did more than that; if it wasn't for him, I would not be running for Senate and my campaign would be over.

I had no illusions that this was going to be easy; I was seen by many as a threat. My secret service guy—a former secret service agent who stays with me at all times at these events—said to me, "Everett, the target on your back just got real big. If you don't get out of this race, they're going to force you out. Those private investigators are going to hound you. Trust me." I was not ready nor willing to quit.

Quietly and anonymously, out of the blue, the list and other information arrived on my desk. Despite the odds against me, I was still in the running. I still had a chance of winning. If there is one lesson I have learned in life, it is that no matter how bad the odds or how impossible the obstacles are to overcome, do what you believe is right.

You will be surprised how much you can achieve.

DANGEROUS LIAISONS

The Republican Committee Chairmen list was not the only surprise that emerged from the Berks County Republican Committee spring dinner. After making my presentation, I was approached by two people—Mark Still and Velma Anne Ruth—from the Patriot Caucus. At the time, I thought they were aligned with the Patriots of Lancaster County, a Republican-backed organization. Ruth told me the Patriot Caucus was pro-national security and they needed my help advancing their mission to protect the USA. After exchanging business cards and contact information, Ruth told me she would reach out to me in about a week. She indicated that Senator Doug Mastriano, US Representative for Pennsylvania's 33rd district, might need help.

Later that evening, she arranged an introduction.

A week later, a phone conversation occurred between Still, Ruth, and myself. The call started with Velma stating there was a national security risk posed by the Biden administration. She said an "audit" of the Pennsylvania election results was critical so that the "true" president, Donald

Trump, could be reinstated. That set off alarm bells in my head. She went on to state that the Patriot Caucus recruited former domestic and foreign intelligence agents for their cause. *Recruiting foreign agents is in itself a national security risk.* By now, the alarm bells were ringing really loudly. She wanted my company, Tactical Rabbit, to provide intelligence services. I asked if she was looking for opposition research, and she said that no, they wanted actionable intelligence (dirt) so they could "move" congressmen, judges, elected officials, and the like in favor of the audit. In other words: *blackmail.*

I asked about her boss, and she said he was General Michael Flynn. I could have said no and walked away, but my private intelligence training told me to play along and see how this played out.

A few days later, I received a call from Al Hartman, a billionaire real estate mogul and Republican donor. I had never met him but, through mutual contacts, we had spoken a number of times about campaign donations. During one of those conversations, he had mentioned he wanted to introduce me to General Flynn and a man named "Kevin" from the American First Movement. To that end, he'd invited me to the Ziklag Conference.

Before I knew it, he was calling to tell me he needed Tactical Rabbit expertise to push for the election audit. He told me he would put me in contact with Ivan Raiklin, and then he proceeded to patch the call through to him and left the call.

Raiklin, as I was to discover, was a multifaceted character—a former Green Beret, attorney, Republican candidate for the US Senate, and entrepreneur. He began our conversation—or, more accurately, his interrogation—by asking about my security classification. He then stopped the telephone call and began texting me questions about my family, associations, and other matters. He suggested we meet in Washington, DC, in June—a meeting that was subsequently put on hold.

The next day, he texted me, saying he wanted me to give a speech to the Patriot Caucus in Lancaster, Pennsylvania. He then patched a telephone call through to Ruth and Still to coordinate. The plan was for Ruth to come listen to the speech and then give me the name of the target. It had reached the point where it was time to contact the authorities.

I called the Head of a Field Office for the FBI. They informed me there was "no time to scramble," that I needed to do what I needed to do while not breaking any laws. This left me in a precarious place; I could give the speech in Lancaster, which totally undermined my own values and beliefs—but if I refused, I would never find out who the target was. In the end, I decided to give the speech, drafted to appease the operatives of the Patriot Caucus—in essence, undermining everything I had stood for.

Ruth arrived at the event wearing a full paramilitary uniform. I walked over to greet her as she was speaking with a former congressional candidate for the Pennsylvania 1st District. We took a photo together, then Ruth pulled me aside and got down to business. She took out her iPad and showed me a list of targets. I asked which target they wanted me to focus on, and she said Congressman Brian Fitzpatrick, a moderate Republican to push toward an audit and an "enemy of Flynn" due to his public, corruption-specialized FBI service. Then she added, "We will accomplish the mission by any means necessary, including the use of domestic terrorism." Senator Toomey was a secondary target, with less of an emphasis than Fitzpatrick. I sent all relevant information to the FBI every chance I could while at the event. About a week later, I reached out to the head of the Pennsylvania GOP, requesting a meeting. The following day, I received a message from the general counsel for the Pennsylvania GOP, asking me to call him. I told him of the threat to Congressman Fitzpatrick. He replied, "We will take care of it."

They did nothing.

Where did all this leave me? As a man in an all-out war, fighting for democracy, with a giant target now on my back.

BECOMING A TACTICAL RABBIT

I am now in my mid-thirties. I've learned, from all of the experiences I've written about in this book, that I am not the worthless loser I always saw in the mirror. I failed at putting a HSBC banker in jail. I failed at winning the US Senate election. I failed to earn the approval of the people I admired most. I have failed time and time again. And I certainly did not make the significant, positive difference I sought out to make.

I wanted to save lives. I wanted to shut down a bank that was sponsoring terrorism. I wanted to storm into Washington as a young, enthusiastic, sincere senator who actually cared and help my constituents. I failed at all of the above. My path to a long road of very public failures all started when I was twenty-five years old, when I sent that first email to the CIA.

But there is a major difference between then and now. I can look myself in the mirror with honor and give myself a little smile. It doesn't matter that I am basically an all-out failure. What matters is that I fought and that I continue to fight. Every day, I set a new goal. I keep getting knocked down

DARK MONEY AND PRIVATE SPIES

only to get back up. I no longer care what others think. I don't seek approval anymore.

Read this very carefully: *If you seek approval, then you will never be able to fight.* Seeking approval means that your actions are influenced by what the masses think. A true fighter finds his or her *why* and gets in that ring with only one determined focus—to win. It doesn't matter if you win or lose the fight. Just by fighting, just by holding that protest sign, just by trying to better society by helping one person breathe easier, you make a bold statement. A leader must lead and be the first one to charge into battle. A leader doesn't check the polls to see if his or her actions are in line with public opinion. Once you find your *why*, you have to ignore everyone else and fight.

For years, I searched for my purpose. I tried to find it in the outside world. I even looked for it in others. But purpose can only be found inside you. It is coded in your DNA. You may not be able to define your purpose right away, but trust me, you are born with it. Life just pulls it out of you. Life shines a light on your *why* whether you like it or not. Deep down, in any situation, you know in your gut what you have to do. You know what you stand for. You know who you are. And you can't let yourself be suppressed by the bullshit opinions of others.

I sat in a room with hundreds of people at HSBC, all looking at similar alerts to mine. Other people saw the same criminally manipulated Wire Filter that I did. I was no genius. Why do you think I was the only one out of hundreds of people at HSBC to open my mouth and fight management so they would stop the terrorist wires? Why was I the only person to report the treason and criminal activity to the Feds?

I blew the whistle on HSBC because, inside, I had already found my *why*. The HSBC scandal simply brought my purpose to light.

If you are reading this book and don't know what your *why* is, just listen to your gut. Listen to your soul and figure out your

DNA. Your *why* is a feeling. And it has an internal, gravitational pull. It will clarify as you are faced with the harsh realities of life and call you out when you forget what's truly important. So many of us have become money zombies. We chase the buck at any cost. Is money important? Of course, it is. We need it to live, and there is nothing wrong with having tons of money. If you can become a millionaire, go for it, but let your purpose guide you.

America is deeply embroiled in a terrible war, but I'm not referring to the war on terrorism. There is a much more insidious, subtler battle in which we are engaged—the war against apathy.

Most people don't care. The biggest challenge our nation faces is that of not caring. This apathy is at the root of many of our problems. We live in an era where "too big to fail" also means "too big to jail." When we turn our backs on the American ideals of integrity, freedom, honor, loyalty, justice, and truth, we embrace apathy.

But the minute you care about something, you become part of the solution. It doesn't matter what your politics are or where you come from, please care about *something*. Don't be like the HSBC bankers who just took a check with numb souls, sending Americans to their deaths with the click of a mouse. Don't be that congressman who said to me, "Make them think that you care." Don't be like former Senator Toomey, who takes campaign donations despite a major conflict of interest from a bank that admitted to treason.

I have learned through all of my hardships that there is always a way. There is always a solution. There is always a right answer—if you just care. You just have to ask the right questions and have the guts to do whatever is necessary to reach your goal. As long as you listen to yourself and are guided by your *why*, not the opinions of others, you will make it. You will make it financially, spiritually, and honorably.

Leaders are not born leaders. A leader is created based on the decisions made in each and every life event. If you're in a place in your life where you feel you have hit rock bottom, then read this very carefully: *muster the courage to venture down the rabbit hole!* You may not know where you will end up. But I can promise you that you will not be at the same rock bottom point you are now. Pick yourself up off of the floor and make a move. Take action. Become a Tactical Rabbit, a creature of pure goodness and innocence that possesses the ability to passionately fight and strategically maneuver. A Tactical Rabbit will jump right down the rabbit hole, having no idea where it will go. A Tactical Rabbit does what most people will never do in their entire lives: *face the unknown with courage, faith, and caring.*

APPENDIX: HSBC EVIDENCE

The evidence I submitted to the United States government proves that HSBC Bank USA is continuing to violate the Bank Secrecy Act of 1970, the Trading with the Enemy Act, and the International Emergency Economic Powers Act. The United States government placed HSBC on a cease-and-desist order in 2010. This means that the bank had one year to clean up its act or face criminal prosecution.

I was hired to "solve" HSBC's downward spiral. It is important to note that the $1.92 billion fine against HSBC did not include my evidence. The $1.92 billion fine was for the crimes HSBC committed up until 2010, not after. My intelligence and evidence showed how HSBC willfully violated the law in an attempt to deceive the government that it was complying with the cease and desist order. The evidence I submitted to the government was for new legal and criminal action against the bank. HSBC Bank USA was never held accountable for the evidence I submitted to the government and was not considered in the design of the deferred prosecution agreement.

The following are excerpts are from the official legal submission on March 11, 2013, to the United States government made on my behalf by my legal team.

Stern discovered specific illegal acts of money laundering activity, concerted efforts designed to dupe the government into believing that HSBC was in compliance with the 2010 cease and desist order and federal anti-money laundering laws and regulations when it was not, rules and incentives that created a general corporate culture that elevated bank profits from suspicious money laundering activity over compliance with the law, internal mechanisms designed to sweep potentially illegal money laundering activity under the rug before it could be properly investigated and reported to authorities, and the presence of gross conflicts of interest. The illegal conduct resulted in HSBC's blatant participation in, and enabling of, drug trafficking, terrorist activities, and the channeling of money to sanctioned regimes abroad. Stern reported his findings to his superiors at HSBC and was at various times ignored, taunted, ridiculed, and ultimately forced out. Stern also reported this information to the CIA and the FBI.

Although HSBC entered into five Settlement Agreements with five different U.S. government agencies on December 11, 2012, pursuant to which HSBC agreed to pay $1.92 billion in fines and penalties, those Settlement Agreements do not release the specific illegal conduct Stern complains of and reports herein, and pertain generally to conduct that occurred prior to Stern's employment with HSBC.

Startlingly, those Settlement Agreements cite HSBC's cooperation and remediation efforts as the basis for leniency in the terms imposed. Complainant's discoveries of continued intentional illegal conduct, detailed below, demonstrate the extent to which those five government agencies were duped by HSBC. It is also worth noting that the fines and penalties imposed on HSBC represent a mere four weeks of profits for this banking behemoth. The U.S. Senate Permanent Subcommittee on Investigations held a hearing on July 13, 2012 regarding HSBC's conduct and issued a HSBC Case History Report on July 17, 2012.

Although HSBC executives met with the subcommittee prior to the hearing to make the case that it had implemented strong reforms since receiving the 2010 cease and desist order, Stern uncovered evidence that some of these reforms were entirely bogus and, indeed, only worked to allow HSBC to increase its illegal conduct and its profits derived therefrom.

Complainant Stern was hired as part of HSBC's effort to comply with these two cease and desist orders, and began working as an Anti-Money Laundering (AML) Officer at HSBC on October 18, 2010. He was appointed to the Target Monitoring Team and the High-Risk Alert Team, where his duties included investigating suspicious banking activity as part of HSBC's Anti-Money Laundering Program and investigating bank customers to ensure they did not do business with certain excluded countries. He was named as the department specialist on Middle Eastern transactions.

When Stern started at HSBC in October of 2010, there were approximately 15-20 compliance officers. At the time of his departure in November of 2012, there were approximately 300 AML compliance officers. However, these new compliance officers were woefully inadequate and unqualified to fulfill their duties. To fill the cubicles in its AML compliance program and to dupe the federal government into believing it was complying with the October 2010 Cease and Desist Orders, HSBC sold its credit card division to Capital One, freed up hundreds of debt collectors and customer service agents from its New Castle, DE call center who had no finance or AML experience and generally only a high school diploma, and hired 300 of them to work as AML compliance officers. HSBC paid these former debt collectors and customer-service agents as much as $55,000 per year, and as a result, retained an enormous amount of leverage over them and their work product

HSBC maintained a computer system infrastructure called CAMP ("Customer Account Monitoring Program") which stored all of the bank's transactions, including all wire transfers of money on behalf of all of its own banking customers and customers of its correspondent banks. A separate computer program, called the Alert Monitoring System, monitored CAMP and sent out an Alert, which notified AML Compliance Officers of suspicious activity regarding a transaction, such as a bank customer sending numerous small dollar wire transfers to multiple beneficiaries in countries designated by the U.S. Department of Treasury's Office of Foreign Assets Control (OFAC) as subject to sanctions (e.g., Iran, Cuba, Sudan, Libya and Burma). The Alert Monitoring System was replaced in the spring of 2011 by a new program called NORKOM, which similarly triggered Alerts. There were three possible dispositions of an Alert. The first was that an AML Compliance Officer would review an Alert and clear it, which would close any inquiry into the underlying transaction that gave rise to the Alert. To close an Alert, the investigator was required to write a narrative that identified some factual information about the entity and/or transaction in question that mitigated any risk posed by that Alert. As discussed below, HSBC used tremendous pressure and offered incentives for AML Officers to close as many Alerts as quickly as possible, to ensure the bank's profits from the underlying transactions. The second disposition was that the Alert would be escalated to a Suspicious Activity Report (SAR), which was sent to Director of Compliance and to the Treasury Department. Before such escalation occurred, a Request for Information (RFI) would be sent to the correspondent bank for more information about the transaction. The third disposition was that the Alert would be placed "on watch." This meant that the Alert was not suspicious enough to be escalated to a SAR, but sufficiently suspicious such that the next time an Alert was generated that referenced the same entity, the investigator would be notified that there was a prior suspicious alert. OFAC maintained a list of regimes, terrorists, international narcotics traffickers, and persons engaged in activities related to the proliferation of weapons of mass destruction. HSBC installed a Wire Filter System that contained all of the names on the OFAC list and was intended to halt any wire transfers or any other flow of funds to or from any OFAC listed person or entity.

Entities that were the subject of HSBC Suspicious Activity Reports (SARs) were also entered into HSBC's Wire Filter System.

During the course of his employment, Stern discovered the following HSBC illegal activities, which he promptly reported to both HSBC senior management and U.S. government officials:

In November 2010, Stern discovered that Crossbar FX Ltd., a Money Servicing Business (MSB) based in the UK, was sending large amounts of money (through low dollar amount transaction under the $10,000 trigger) through HSBC to numerous individuals and entities in the Middle East and China. Crossbar FX claimed on its website to have a banking relationship with HSBC. To confirm his findings, Stern pretended to be an importer/exporter and phoned Crossbar FX. He spoke with a man who identified himself as the owner and stated that Crossbar was a one-man operation that exchanged currency and that could provide lower exchange rates than banks. Stern searched the HSBC CAMP system and found that Crossbar FX had used coding on its wire transfers designed to evade HSBC's Alert Monitoring System and had funneled over $40 million through HSBC to other MSBs in China and the Middle East. This is against AML regulations, which require the bank to know exactly who both the originator and beneficiary of a wire transfer was.

Having a MSB on either end of a wire transfer is the paradigm of a classic money laundering scheme because it hides the true identities of both the originator and the beneficiary. Stern immediately reported this to his superiors.

In addition, on November 7, 2010, Stern sent an email from his personal email account to a CIA recruiter to report this discovery.

In December 2010, Stern discovered that a Canadian shipping company was sending suspicious wires through HSBC to other shipping companies. Every bank client has a KYC (Know Your Customer) form on file at the bank. It contains summary information about the client, including a description, location information, ownership, contact information, etc. It was Stern's job to investigate both transactions and customers for any suspicious activities or ties. If Stern thought there was an issue with a bank client, he was to review the KYC and determine whether a SAR on that client should be filed. As part of his investigation of the KYC of this Canadian shipping company, Stern telephoned the shipping company and pretended to be an importer/exporter trying to get bullets into Iran, and explained that due to OFAC regulations he could not do so.

The company offered to help and to have someone waiting at the airport in Tehran to unload the cargo and see that it gets to its proper destination in Iran. This was a violation of AML laws and regulations—the bank could not have a client that did business or otherwise had any ties to any OFAC-listed country, including Iran. Stern wanted to draft a SAR, which would have been sent to the Treasury Department, and immediately notified his superiors of these facts. All of the Canadian shipping company's bank transactions were subsequently approved. Stern promptly reported this information to the CIA.

In January 2011, Stern discovered that HSBC was allowing hundreds of millions of dollars in terrorist funds to move through HSBC and Standard Chartered Bank (a correspondent bank of HSBC) from Africa to Beirut, Lebanon. The money was originating from Kairaba Supermarkets and Shopping Centres (an OFAC-listed sanctioned company) in Gambia and going to Tajco, a company based in Beirut (also an OFAC-listed sanctioned company) that owns a majority interest in Kairaba. Tajco is run by the Tajideen Brothers, OFAC-listed persons who the U.S. State Department has determined are terrorists and the financiers of Hezbollah. Although Kairaba and Tajco had been entered into the Wire Filter System, those names had been misspelled.

Because the Wire Filter only reads exact names and does not pick up misspellings or any slight variation in the name, these illegal money transfers were allowed to go through. Stern immediately notified management of this problem, but no corrections were made in the Wire Filter. Thus, Hezbollah was allowed to continue to launder money through HSBC. Stern believes that this illegal activity still continues to this day. Stern promptly reported this information to the CIA.

In March 2011, Stern discovered that Sharbatly Fruit, a Saudi Arabian fruit distribution company banking with SABB (a correspondent bank of HSBC formerly known as The Saudi British Bank), was sending millions of dollars to an individual in Yemen. Stern researched the individual and found that he was a leading party member of the Yemini Party of Reform, frequently called Islah or Al-Islah, which is the main opposition party in Yemen that was created in September 1990 by Yemeni members of the Muslim Brotherhood. Because Saudi Arabia was labeled a high-risk country by HSBC and because the funds were going to a Yemeni political person (in industry parlance, known as a PEP, or "Politically Exposed Person"), this was a highly suspicious activity that should have risen to the level of a SAR. Stern outlined his concerns in a written Alert narrative requesting that it be elevated to a SAR and attached all supporting documentation, including articles from the Brookings Institute and other academic articles proving the link to the Muslim Brotherhood. Stern was scolded for using the words "possible terrorist financing" and "suspicious activity" in his report. His request for a SAR was denied and all of Sharbatly Fruit's transactions were approved. Stern promptly reported this information to the CIA.

In June of 2011, as the specialist on the Middle East, Stern discovered that a number of the former HSBC debt collectors who were appointed AML Compliance Officers were approving transactions going to foundations in the Gaza Strip. Stern reported this to his superiors, and warned that Hamas, which the U.S. State Department has deemed a terrorist organization, is the elected government of Gaza and that this money could be used to fund terrorism. He did so by sending an email titled "Compliance Error." Subsequently, a higher up pulled Stern into a conference room and threatened to fire him, stating, "Do you know what would happen if the government found out about the Compliance Error email? They would shut us down. Do you fucking understand we are under a cease and desist order and you are putting in writing that we have a compliance error!? ▪▪▪▪▪▪▪▪ would fire you in two seconds if he found out about this." When Stern tried to explain the situation to ▪▪▪▪▪▪▪▪▪▪, ▪▪▪▪▪▪▪▪▪ stated, "Hamas is not a terrorist organization—they were elected to power." Stern reminded ▪▪▪▪▪▪▪▪▪ that even though Hamas was elected, it was still considered a terrorist organization by the U.S. government and was on the OFAC list. Nothing was done and all wires into Gaza were approved. Stern promptly reported this information to the CIA.

Currently, HSBC Senior Vice President ▪▪▪▪▪▪▪, under orders from Chief Compliance Officer ▪▪▪▪▪▪, is now setting up operations in Sri Lanka for AML Investigations to be conducted overseas by foreign nationals. This is highly improper as HSBC itself rates Sri Lanka as a high-risk country for money laundering. It leaves HSBC's AML functions open to being infiltrated, improperly influenced and exploited by corrupt local employees.

Recently, Stern was told by a senior member of the HSBC AML compliance program team that in the summer of 2012 and as a favor to HSBC Hong Kong, Senior Vice President of Financial Intelligence ▪▪▪▪▪▪ altered the Wire Filter System to remove certain OFAC listed entities, which allowed millions of dollars of wire transactions initiated by HSBC Hong Kong to go through. These were transactions that had previously been held up by the Wire Filter System because the money was either going to or coming from an OFAC-listed entity. ▪▪▪▪▪▪ sent an internal HSBC email to AML staff outlining her actions.

HSBC created a culture of evading AML rules and regulations among its AML compliance program investigators by encouraging, motivating and, rewarding those investigators to close as many Alerts as possible (and thus ensure the bank's profits), regardless of the circumstances and red flags present in the transaction. Investigators were specifically pushed not to identify and eliminate transactions with suspicious activity, because eliminating such transactions would decrease bank profits. The goal was to close the Alerts and green light the underlying transactions and avoid elevating the Alert to a Suspicious Activity Report (SAR). Although federal regulations are designed to reduce illegal money laundering and prohibit such financing transactions, the bank that is charged with ferreting out and voiding these transactions makes more money if those transactions slide through the bank undetected. Rather than honor its regulatory obligations to detect and eliminate illegal transactions, HSBC erected a facade of compliance efforts while encouraging its compliance personnel to actually approve the illegal transactions. HSBC created this culture in the following way.

AML team management set minimum Alert clearing goals to keep production high. During the summer of 2011, management set the weekly minimum of Alert clearings at 72 Alerts per week per investigator. The investigators were flabbergasted by this announcement and openly protested, saying it could not be done. •••••••• replied, "Find a way." Indeed, Stern was specifically told by Senior Vice President ••••••••, "You have to find a way to mitigate risk—you have to find a way." •••••••• was instructing Stern to find anything that he could use to show that the risk of a transaction being related to money laundering was mitigated such that the corresponding Alert could be closed.

Management loosened the criteria to clear an Alert when a backlog of Alerts developed, and later reversed course when the backlog subsided. This occurred in February 2011 when •••••••••• sent an email to all the investigators stating that transactions through The Saudi British Bank could be closed or closed on watch without sending a RFI to Saudi British Bank to get more information because Saudi British Bank could be trusted. Any Alert related to Saudi British Bank was automatically cleared, despite the fact that Saudi Arabia was labeled by HSBC as a high-risk country. The same thing happened with HSBC Hong Kong in June 2011.

Management determined and informed the investigators that no investigations were needed for bank-to-bank transfers. As such, Alerts based on such transfers could be automatically closed. Investigators routinely sought out these Alerts to examine because they were the easiest to close. This is a gross violation of AML rules. Just because transfers are from one bank to another does not mean that money isn't being laundered or funneled to terrorist organizations or OFAC-listed entities. Not all foreign banks can be trusted.

On December 11, 2012, HSBC entered into a deferred prosecution agreement ("DPA") pursuant to which the Department of Justice filed a four-count Criminal Information in the United States District Court for the Eastern District of New York and agreed to defer prosecution, and HSBC agreed, among other things, to pay $1.92 billion fines and penalties. The Criminal Information charged the HSBC Parties with the following illegal activity:

> willfully failing to maintain an effective anti-money laundering program, in violation of The Bank Secrecy Act of 1970 (BSA), Title 31, United States Code, section 5318(h) and regulations issued thereunder;
> willfully failing to conduct and maintain due diligence on correspondent bank accounts held on behalf of foreign persons, in violation of the BSA, Title 31, United States Code, Section 5318(i) and regulations issued thereunder; and
> willfully violating and attempting to violate the Trading with the Enemy Act (TWEA), Title 50 United States Code Appendix Sections 3,5,16, and regulations issued thereunder; and willfully violating and attempting to violate the International Emergency Economic Powers Act (IEEPA), Title 50 United States Code Sections 1702 and 1705, and regulations issued thereunder.

The HSBC Group violated IEEPA and TWEA by illegally conducting transactions on behalf of customers in Cuba, Iran, Libya, Sudan, and Burma—all countries that were subject to sanctions enforced by the Office of Foreign Assets Control (OFAC) at the time of the transactions.

HSBC's illegal acts, as set forth in the Statement of Facts attached to the DPA, include:

> lack of an effective anti-money laundering (AML) function in 2006 through 2010 that facilitated the laundering of

at least $881 million in drug proceeds through the U.S. financial system;

failure to adequately monitor over $200 trillion in wire transfers between 2006 and 2009 from customers located in countries that HSBC Bank USA classified as "standard" or "medium" risk;

from the mid-1990s through September 2006, allowing approximately $660 million in OFAC-prohibited transactions to move through the U.S. financial system on behalf of banks located in Cuba, Iran, Libya, Sudan, and Burma, in violation of U.S. economic sanctions; and

from 2006 to 2010, severely understaffing its AML compliance function and failing to implement an anti-money laundering program capable of adequately monitoring suspicious transactions and activities from HSBC Group Affiliates, particularly HSBC Mexico. This included a failure to monitor billions of dollars in purchases of physical U.S. dollars, or "banknotes," from these affiliates.

The December 11, 2012 Settlements do in any way release HSBC's liability for the violations of the BSA, IEEPA and TWEA set forth herein for the following reasons. First, the illegal conduct that Stern complains of herein is not addressed by the Settlement.

Each of the five Settlement Agreements entered into by HSBC on December 11, 2012 contains its own factual findings and release language. Each of those Agreements specifically refers to HSBC conduct that occurred in 2010 or prior, and not during the time period Stern worked at HSBC and independently observed illegal conduct as reported herein. The release language in each of those Agreements, in general, only releases HSBC from liability for conduct that (i) was specifically disclosed to the government agencies, (ii) was set forth in factual findings, and/or (iii) occurred during the time period generally discussed in the factual findings. In fact, the Department of Justice Settlement Agreement with HSBC specifically states that HSBC may still be prosecuted for knowingly and willfully transmitting or approving the transmission of funds to or from OFAC-designated entities, other than for transactions disclosed and documented to the U.S. Thus, the conduct that Stern complains of, which forms the basis of his allegations herein, is not released in the Settlement.

Second, the Settlements relate to conduct that occurred in 2010 and prior, and not to conduct that Stern complains of which occurred after the date Stern began working at HSBC in December 2010.

Thus, there remain viable claims for HSBC's violations of AML laws and regulations beginning in December 2010 and continuing to the present.

Made in United States
North Haven, CT
08 December 2022

27833858R00089